IMAGES
of America

HISTORIC
MAGNOLIA CEMETERY

Serenity could be found in Magnolia Cemetery at the beginning of its centennial year, 1952. Magnolia is the resting place for Baton Rouge citizens of all walks of life, races, religions, and political persuasions. Military veterans from Louisiana who served in wars in America and throughout the world lie peacefully in Magnolia. (Courtesy of the *Advocate*, Baton Rouge.)

ON THE COVER: The main gate on North Nineteenth Street welcomes all who visit. The gate matches the 1909 cast-iron fence made by the R. Pike Company of New Orleans, which surrounds all sides of the cemetery. Behind the entrance stands the Crenshaw Monument, the best-known monument in the cemetery. It depicts the three young Crenshaw children who died of yellow fever in 1858. Magnolia Cemetery was listed in the National Register of Historic Places on January 4, 1985. The plaque is on the right post of the gate. (Photograph by Chip Landry.)

IMAGES
of America

HISTORIC
MAGNOLIA CEMETERY

Chip Landry and Faye Phillips

ARCADIA
PUBLISHING

Published by Arcadia Publishing
Charleston, South Carolina

Printed in the United States of America

Library of Congress Control Number: 2019936588

For all general information, please contact Arcadia Publishing:
Telephone 843-853-2070
Fax 843-853-0044
E-mail sales@arcadiapublishing.com
For customer service and orders:
Toll-Free 1-888-313-2665

Visit us on the Internet at www.arcadiapublishing.com

To all those who work to preserve Magnolia Cemetery.

CONTENTS

ACKNOWLEDGMENTS

The authors wish to thank the Magnolia Cemetery Board of Trustees and Preserve Louisiana for their support of this project and book. We also wish to thank Carolyn Bennett for her help in fact-checking and for proofreading. Melissa Eastin, head of Special Collections, and Emily Ward, digital archivist, East Baton Rouge Parish Library, offered their assistance and support for the project. We appreciate the help of the many librarians, archivists, and individuals who provided images. Unless otherwise noted, all images appear courtesy of Chip Landry.

INTRODUCTION

The interconnection of Baton Rouge families is clearly shown through reading Magnolia Cemetery tombstones. In the Thiel-Nephler family plot in Section No. 1, we can presume that the Nephler family was the reason the Thiel family members are buried there. Emma C. Nephler married Charles Augustus Thiel, and though they lived in New Orleans, their bodies were brought to Magnolia Cemetery to lie next to the members of her family, the Nephlers. The Herron family intermarried with the Bird family, as shown by their graves' locations, and the Wieck and Wax families, as well as the Elam and Day families, also intermarried. Many of the placements of those interred in Magnolia Cemetery can be understood through family relations and genealogy. We connect with the past by bringing a familiarity with our ancestors to life through our cemeteries and their histories.

In 1852, the growing city of Baton Rouge needed a nondenominational public cemetery. Land on the eastern edge of town was purchased from John Christian Buhler Jr. for $3,000 to establish a municipal cemetery of approximately 10 acres. The subtly rolling terrain comprised open agricultural fields dotted with magnolias and cedar stands. Early burials occurred in the western portion, while the eastern portion was planted with corn for many years. The parcel is bounded on the north by Main Street, on the south by Florida Boulevard, to the west by North Nineteenth Street, and to the east by North Twenty-Second Street. The original picket fence from 1869 was replaced in installments with an iron fence, which enclosed the cemetery when it was completed in 1909.

The Nineteenth Street entrance gate bears a decorative iron banner with the cemetery's name. The original drive laid out in 1879 runs east to west and has a gate on North Twenty-Second Street, which is no longer a public entrance, although for many years it was a thoroughfare. Near the cemetery's center, a covered gazebo serves as a gathering place. Large shade trees line the central axis and western perimeter, while smaller flowering trees dot the lawn. Unlike New Orleans cemeteries of this era, burials in Magnolia Cemetery are subterranean, marked with plain tombstones, sarcophagi, blanket stones, or rounded grave covers and a few multiple-person vaults. Occasionally, a grave has a beautifully carved, elaborate monument. Family plots, arranged in an orderly grid, are often enclosed with stone borders, coping, or iron fencing.

Although most of the lots were sold to individuals and benevolent societies, one quarter was set aside as a potters' field for the poor and unknown. Modern tombstones are placed side by side with 19th-century obelisks, carved angels, urns, and lambs. There are numerous politicians and officials who served the city, state, and nation, as well as their families, at rest in Magnolia. Children who died too young, citizens who lived almost a century, men and women soldiers from all American wars, and individuals from all professions and jobs that make a city function, fill Magnolia's quiet plots. Many of these people in life served in fraternal associations, such as the Masons, the Woodmen of the World (WOW), and the Odd Fellows. Symbols of these organizations appear frequently on tombstones. The Masons' most recognizable symbols are the square and compass, which are tools of their trades. However, none can compete with the Woodmen of the World, whose entire headstones are carved to look like tree stumps or logs. Often, the tombstones are inscribed with the epitaph "here rests a Woodman of the World," for the fraternity rules state that Woodmen "do not lie."

Leading Protestant citizens of all races were buried here along with many of other denominations and faiths. When Magnolia Cemetery opened, some caretakers of family cemeteries around Baton Rouge brought bodies there for reinterment. A few graves from the downtown cemetery near the military fort were moved as well. Thus, the earliest death dates for those in Magnolia are from the 1820s, predating the cemetery's creation. For families that own a plot, new burials are allowed when space permits, and 21st-century burials have occurred.

Some of the heaviest fighting waged during the Civil War's Battle of Baton Rouge took place in and near the cemetery on August 5, 1862, and it is the only part of the battleground that is still intact since all other portions now contain commercial and residential buildings. The grave markers, trees, and picket fence surrounding the cemetery were used as cover by both Confederate and Union troops. There were a total of 849 casualties in this significant conflict. Because of the battle, Federal leaders feared the Confederates would next assault New Orleans, so to protect that city, they moved their forces south from Baton Rouge. From August until December 1862, the Confederate forces occupied the town and used the advantage to fortify Port Hudson north of Baton Rouge, thus stopping Federal troops moving northward on the Mississippi River. Although records are unclear, local tradition holds that most of the Confederate dead were buried by Federal troops and/or Baton Rouge citizens in a mass grave. A solid granite stone marks their resting place. Every year, Preserve Louisiana's Magnolia Cemetery Board of Trustees sponsors a Battle of Baton Rouge commemorative ceremony in remembrance of those who died.

Following the Civil War, due to a poor postwar economy, and later, as many of the old families moved away, Magnolia Cemetery fell into disrepair. Local citizens and those with family members buried in Magnolia Cemetery are asked to work with the cemetery board to maintain it. In 1985, Magnolia Cemetery was listed in the National Register of Historic Places. Through this book, we hope to reacquaint Baton Rouge with the cemetery.

Magnolia Cemetery is arranged in six sections with lots for burials. Sections Nos. 1 and 2 both have 91 designated lots. Sections Nos. 3 and 4 each have 157 lots. Section No. 5 has 99 lots, and Section No. 6 has 79 designated lots. Each section is represented by a chapter. The seventh chapter illustrates problems with damage and neglect as well as acknowledgment of some companies that provided tombstones and monuments. Every chapter title is an epitaph from a tombstone.

One

THE NAMELESS ONE

The Crenshaw monument, located in Section No. 1, Plot No. 98, is the best-known monument in the cemetery. The sculpture depicts the faces of three young children who died in the Baton Rouge yellow fever epidemic of 1858. Their parents were Methodist reverend William H. and Mary E. Crenshaw, and they are likely buried beneath their monument.

THE NAMELESS
ONE
19TH. DEC. 1855.

Buried together under the monument with an infant are Fanny Bell Crenshaw (1849–1858), Willie Harney Crenshaw (1851–1858), and Martha "Mattie" Pike Crenshaw (1857–1858). The baby, "the nameless one," was born and died on December 19, 1855. Each side of the monument recognizes one of the children. The memorial was designed and built by a business with the all-inclusive name of Acme Marble Granite Company Builders in New Orleans. The Crenshaw monument was damaged on August 5, 1862, when US and Confederate forces clashed in Magnolia Cemetery. Later, it lost its top finial and was further damaged by a tree falling in a storm. Roselawn Monuments of Baton Rouge and the Foundation for Historical Louisiana restored the memorial.

FANNY BELL.
BORN
7TH. APRIL 1849.
DIED
5TH. JUNE 1858.

CHILDREN OF
WILLIAM H &
MARY E. CRENSHAW.
WILLIE HARNEY.
BORN
31ST. OCT. 1851.
DIED
8TH. JUNE 1858.

The oldest Crenshaw child, 11-year-old Fanny Bell, died on June 5, 1858, and her brother, seven-year-old Willie, died three days later. The family's grief was compounded when nine-year-old Mattie died on October 13 of that year. The Baton Rouge yellow fever epidemic of 1858 was not as severe as future epidemics, such as that of 1878, but many of those who died were the very young, like the Crenshaw children. The columned, domed pedestal frames the gentle likenesses of the children. The dome is decorated on top with roses and other flowers, representing short lives.

MATTIE PIKE,
BORN
20TH. MAY 1857.
DIED
13TH. OCT. 1858.

Andrew David Lytle (1834–1917) took this photograph of his family's Magnolia Cemetery plot in 1890. Upon his death, he was also buried there. Other family members interred in the plot include his children, Andrew S. (1857–1859), William Lundy Lytle (1862–1868), and Howard Lytle (1870–1915), and wife, Mary Ann Lundy Lytle (1836–1898), as well as other relatives. In 1901, Lytle served as the secretary for the board of directors of the city cemetery. Sadly, Lytle also took the photograph below of his son Andrew on his deathbed. Andrew S. Lytle was born shortly after his parents arrived in Baton Rouge. Of his three sons and one daughter, only daughter Ethel (1871–1951) outlived Lytle. (Both, courtesy of the Andrew D. Lytle Collection, Louisiana and Lower Mississippi Valley Collections, Louisiana State University [LSU] Libraries.)

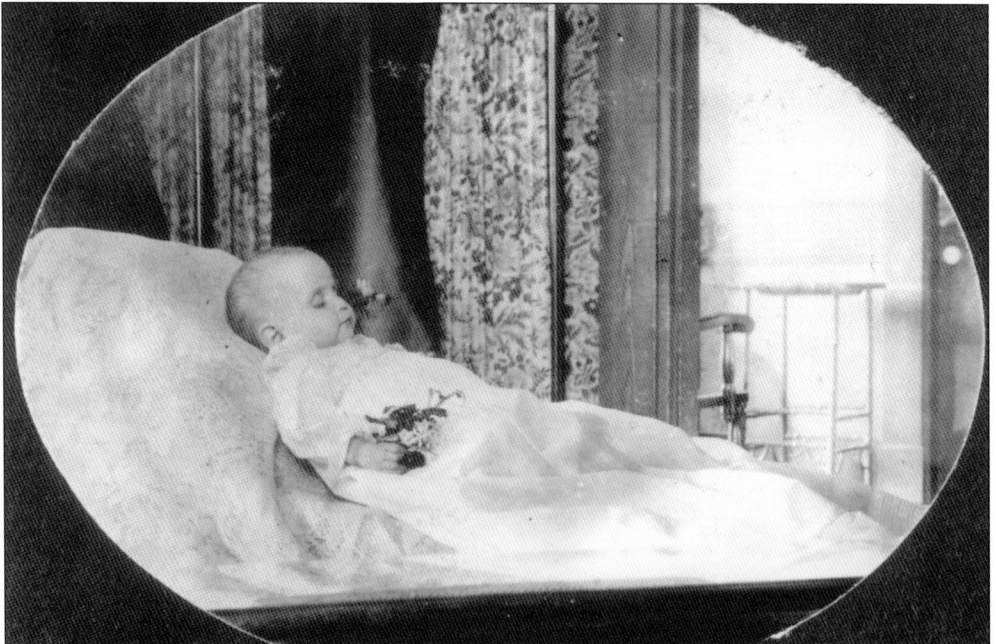

The monument for Joanna Painter Fox Waddill (1838–1899), found in Section No. 1, Lot No. 22, has the following inscription: "Hospital Matron 1862–65. C.S.A. Camp 17. U.C.V." Over time, Waddill has gained the nickname "Confederate Florence Nightingale." Her tombstone shows a Confederate flag surrounded by an ivy wreath. At 22 years old, Joanna met her future husband when they were both serving in Confederate hospitals in Mississippi. She and George Daniel Waddill (1836–1904) came to live in his hometown, Baton Rouge, where they owned and operated a drugstore on Main Street. She helped create the Confederate Memorial Association of Baton Rouge, which became the United Daughters of the Confederacy. Named for her after her death, the Baton Rouge Joanna Waddill Chapter No. 294, United Daughters of the Confederacy (UDC), celebrated 120 years on April 5, 2019. (Right, courtesy of the Waddill Family Papers, Louisiana and Lower Mississippi Valley Collections, LSU Libraries.)

The Scott family in Section No. 1, Lot No. 57, were originally buried on the grounds of their plantation, Scotland Farm, a beautiful spot on the bluffs of the Mississippi River north of Baton Rouge. In 1839, Dr. William Bernard Scott purchased the property, then known as the Monte Sano Plantation, from Lelia Skipwith Robertson (1804–1844). Both Lelia's father, Fulwar Skipwith (1765–1839), and her husband, Gov. Thomas Boling Robertson (1779–1828), had lived there. The Scotland Farm property was sold to nonfamily owners around 1914 and became the location of Southern University. Scott's Bluff is a historic part of Southern University, and the town that grew around the university was named Scotlandville. Scott family members were reinterred at Magnolia Cemetery. Their deaths and first burials predate the opening of Magnolia Cemetery in 1852. John A. Scott (1821–1825) and Robert S. Scott (1826–1837) are two children remembered along with six other family members on a single obelisk.

Surrounding the Scott family's obelisk is a lovely fence with symbols of eternal life, such as lilies and unbroken circles. Over time, the fence has been damaged, and parts of it are lost. While the wrought iron fence that encloses the whole cemetery is maintained, few of the fences around family plots show signs of permanent maintenance.

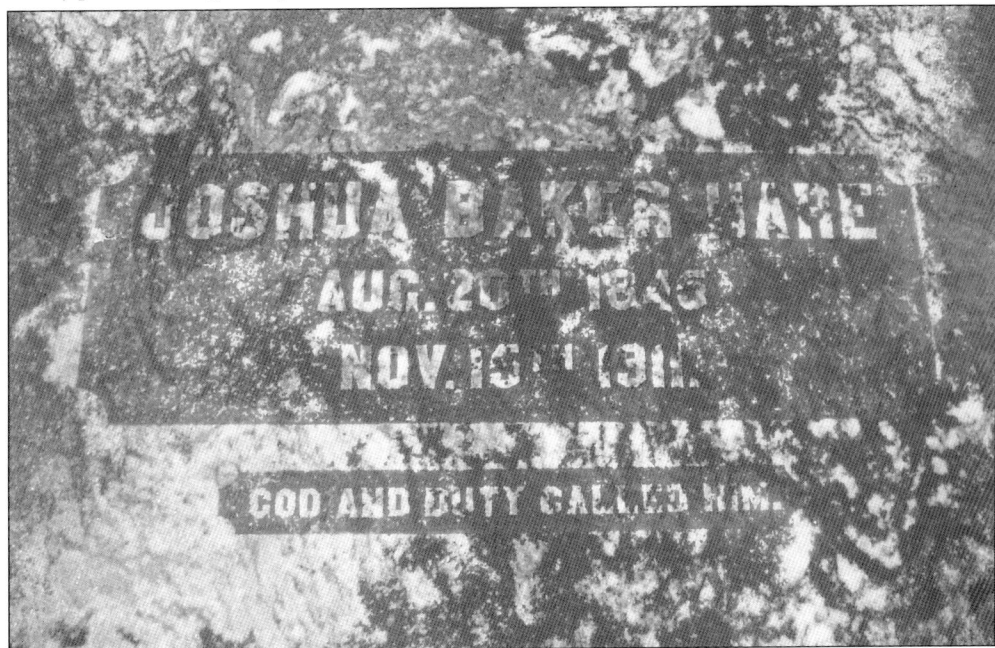

Joshua Baker Hare (1846–1911), found in Section No. 1, Lot No. 6, was a private in Company E, 5th Louisiana Infantry, and Vinson's Scouts, Louisiana Cavalry, during the Civil War. There is also a Confederate memorial gravestone, with a Southern Cross of Honor, for Hare near his tombstone. His wife, Clara Anderson Hare (1851–1928), is buried nearby.

This photograph was taken of Joshua Baker Hare when he became the Baton Rouge police chief in 1888. He served until 1911, when he was shot and killed while trying to disarm a drunken police officer. He had been with the police department for 25 years. The local newspaper estimated that 3,000 mourners attended his funeral. (Courtesy of the Baton Rouge Police Department.)

Henry Wolf (1864–1901), Section No. 1, Lot No. 55, and his family immigrated from Germany after the Civil War. They established a beloved bakery, Wolf's Sunbeam Baker. Henry and his brother William Leonard Wolf (1857–1911) learned to bake from their parents. Many remember the bakery's aroma in the air, along with Wolf's bread wrappers, which could often be exchanged for prizes.

WOLF

WILLIAM WOLF
JULY 30, 1857
APR 1, 1911

SARAH KELLUM
FEB 7, 1859
DEC 29, 1953

WILLIAM L. WOLF
DIED FEB. 13, 1870
AGE 44

ANNA M. WOLF
DIED JAN. 31, 1892
AGE 68

HENRY WOLF
DIED NOV. 7, 1901
AGE 38

LEVI WOLF
DIED NOV. 1, 1892
AGE 4

CATHARINE FLECK
DIED NOV. 9, 1888 AGE 72

William Stewart Booth (1839–1903), Section No. 1, Lot No. 30, was a second lieutenant in Company B, 1st Louisiana Cavalry, during the Civil War. As is common for early military burials, Booth's grave has a headstone and a footstone. Many of the tombstones for Confederate military members have the outline of the Southern Cross of Honor. His wife, Elvira "Ella" Benton Booth (1842–1918), and five of their children are buried with him.

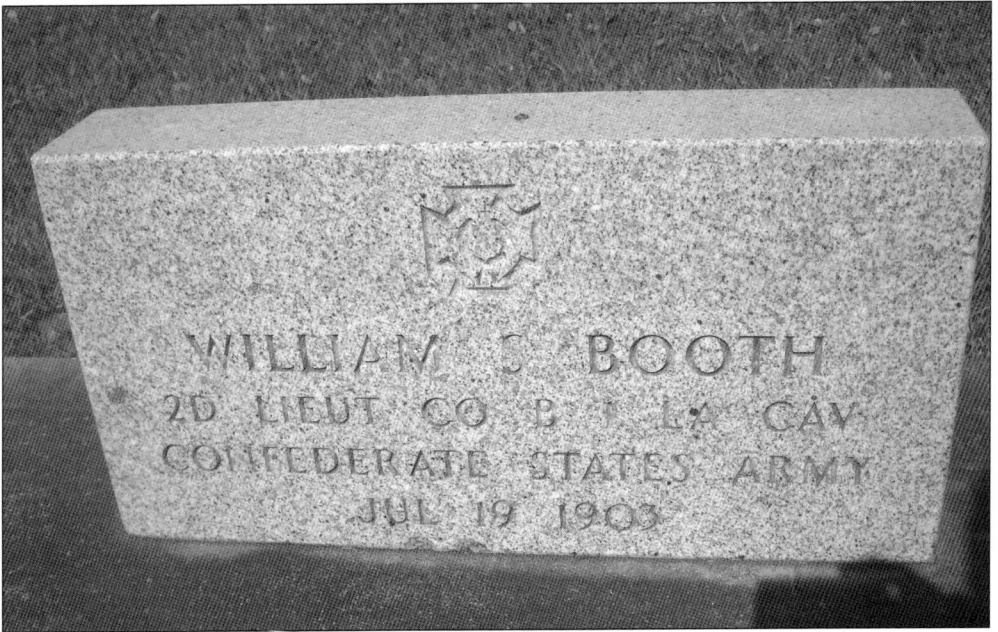

After the war, Booth owned Hundred Oaks Plantation, which included the land around the current Perkins Road overpass. At his business in downtown Baton Rouge near Third Street, Booth sold harnesses, saddles, bridles, and an assortment of saddle hardware. In 1876, Booth and his partner, Thomas H. Hall, invented an improved faucet for beer and liquor casks. Booth was mayor of Baton Rouge in 1883–1884.

Section No. 1 of Magnolia Cemetery sits at the corner of Main and North Nineteenth Street, which was once named Dufrocq Street for former mayor John Dufrocq. Early maps of the cemetery property include the names of the original 12 purchasers of lots. It was arranged into six sections that contained as few as 79 separate lots and as many as 157 separate lots. As early as 1854, burial lots were purchased from the original owners by numerous families, benevolent associations, individuals, businesses, and institutions. The Baton Rouge Female Orphan Asylum purchased Lot No. 69, where babies such as Sallie Shummi, who died at eight months old in May 1901, are buried. Placed throughout Section No. 1 are benches for bereaved visitors or those needing a place to rest or reflect. All variations of tombstones, grave markers, fences, and unique monuments, such as the Crenshaw monument, are found throughout Section No. 1.

William George Randolph Sr. (1842–1894), Section No. 1, Lot No. 55, was a sergeant in Company B, 7th Louisiana Infantry, and a prisoner of war during the Civil War. His headstone shows the Southern Cross of Honor. His wife, Minna Matta Randolph (1843–1926), and one daughter, Sydney M. Randolph (1889–1964), are also buried here. He and Minna had 13 children.

DIED.

In this city, Tuesday, July 31, 1894, at 4 o'clock a. m.,

W. G. RANDOLPH,

aged **51** years and **8** months.

Friends and acquaintances of the family are respectfully invited to attend the funeral, which will take place from the residence on Lafayette street, this (TUESDAY) evening at 4:30 o'clock. Interment at Magnolia Cemetery.

The officers and members of St. James Lodge, No. 49, F. and A. M., are notified to meet at their lodge hall this (Tuesday) evening at 4 o'clock, to assist in paying the last sad tribute of respect to their departed brother. Sojourning brethren in good standing are fraternally invited to attend.
By order of the W. M.   M. GRANARY, Secretary.

HEADQUARTERS CAMP NO. 17, U.C. V.,
July 31, 1894.
The member of Camp No. 17, U. C. V., are hereby notified to meet at Headquarters at 4 o'clock p. m. to attend the funeral of our late comrade, W. G. Randolph.
By order of First Lieutenant Commander.
F. W. HℓROMAN, Adjutant.

The members of the Fire Department are hereby notified to assemble at their respective halls this (Tuesday) evening at 4 o'clock, to attend the funeral of W. G. Randolph, except member of Pelican Hook and Ladder Company No. 1.
SIMON BLOCK, Pelican Hook and Ladder No. 1.
HENRY GIMLER, Secretary Independence No. 2.
RYAN AMISS, Secretary Washington No. 3.
LAZARD BLUM, Secretary Jackson No. 4.
S. FEARSON, Secretary Schloss No. 5
S. D. SCHOLCRAFT, Secretary Loucks No. 6.
B. J. GOODMAN, Secretary Washington No. 1.

BATON ROUGE, LA., July 31, 1894.

Randolph's funeral notice lists three organizations that were important to him. He was a member of the St. James Lodge No. 47, Free and Accepted Masons, and a retired member of Pelican Hook and Ladder Company No. 1, Baton Rouge Fire Department. The members of Camp No. 17, United Confederate Veterans, were also encouraged to attend. (Courtesy of Baton Rouge Funeral Notices, Louisiana and Lower Mississippi Valley Collections, LSU Libraries.)

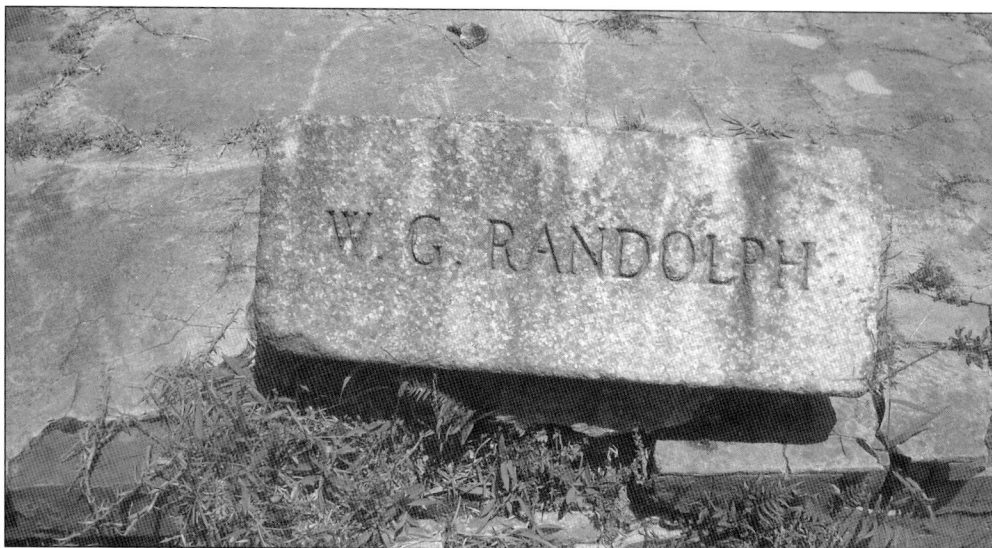

William George Randolph Sr.'s apparent footstone was perhaps his only stone until the headstone in the previous image could be acquired. He was a prominent businessman and also served as parish treasurer. Randolph was killed in an altercation on Third Street with Dr. King Holt who had previously served as his medical doctor. Holt is also buried in Magnolia in Section No. 2.

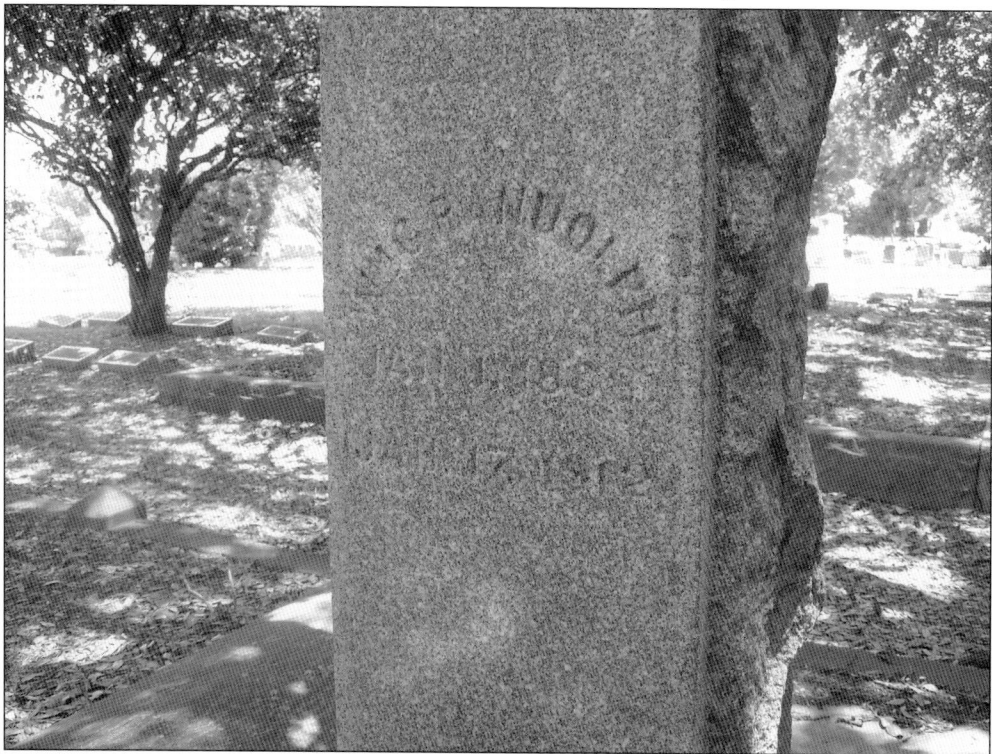

William George Randolph Jr. (1868–1912) was East Baton Rouge Parish sheriff at the time of his death. Randolph, a supporter of Leon Jastremski's white separatist politics, ran for sheriff with Jastremski's gubernatorial party ticket in 1903. Randolph also led the local Woodmen of the World and, as did his father, served as parish treasurer.

Andrew Stewart Herron (1823–1882), Section No. 1, Lot No. 58, was a lawyer who served as a major in Company B, 7th Louisiana Infantry, and was appointed colonel and judge of Mobile's military court in 1863. A native of Nashville, Tennessee, he held the office of Louisiana secretary of state and was elected state attorney general in 1865. Herron was elected to the US Congress in 1882 but died before being seated. He is buried near his daughter Mary S. Herron Bird (1853–1915). At the apex of Herron's gravestone is the prominent Knights Templar symbol of a cross and crown. The statue of a Confederate soldier that once stood at the corner at North and Third Streets was completed in 1890 and represented all who served. According to local lore, the face of the statue was made in Andrew S. Herron's likeness. His epitaph reads: "Mark the perfect man, and / behold the upright: for the / end of that man is peace."

In 1950, Mary Bird Perkins (1927–1966) was one of the first female graduates of the Louisiana State University Law Center. Her father, Paul Dorsey Perkins (1887–1978), worked to establish the Mary Bird Perkins Cancer Center at Our Lady of the Lake Hospital. He also purportedly established a fund for perpetual care of Mary's grave. The lovely wrought iron fence around the Bird-Herron lot came from Perkins's home on Fourth Street. Neither the graves nor the fence show evidence of being cared for as Perkins supposedly intended. Mary's maternal grandmother and namesake, Mary Herron Bird (1853–1915), was the daughter of Andrew S. Herron. Four other Bird family members are also buried in the lot.

Wade Hampton Bynum (1868–1946), Section No. 1, Lot No. 70, was the mayor of Baton Rouge from 1903 to 1910. He became mayor again in 1922 when he replaced his brother Turner (1878–1922), who died in office, and was then reelected and served from 1923 to 1941. Bynum led Baton Rouge through times of expansion, issuing bonds to fund paving and sewage projects and to build the municipal docks and city park.

Inside the fence surrounding the Andre family plot, located in Section No. 1, Lot No. 7, are the blanket gravestones of Gabriel Andre (1794–1860) and Margaretha Louisa Rasche Andre (1790–1862) of Germany. Another member of the Andre family, Joseph Andre (1874–1946), has a cross at the top of his tombstone and a Woodmen of the World memorial circle at the bottom. A matching cross is on the headstone of his wife, Emma Wood Andre (1877–1953).

William F. Tunnard (1809–1871), Section No. 1, Lot No. 62, was born in New York City. He owned and operated W.F. Tunnard Carriage and Harness Factory on the southeast corner of Main and North Third Streets. His business was very successful. Tunnard manufactured an assortment of iron items such as balcony railings and fences for cemeteries. At the beginning of the Civil War, he and his sons closed the factory and volunteered to join the Confederate army; he served in Company K, 3rd Louisiana Infantry. He returned to his business at the end of the war. In 1866, son Frederick Devoo Tunnard (1835–1909), Company K, 3rd Louisiana Infantry, took over the business; he is seen at left. Another son, William H. Tunnard (1837–1916), wrote and published *A Southern Record: The History of the Third Regiment Louisiana Infantry*. (Left, courtesy of the State Library of Louisiana.)

LUCRETIA
ARONS
WIFE OF
H. W. JOLLY
DIED
JAN. 24. 1918.
AGE 97 YEARS.

Born in Cincinnati, Ohio, Lucretia Arons Jolly (1820–1918), and her husband, Henry William Jolly (1813–1875), Section No. 1, Lot No. 59, came to Baton Rouge on a flatboat around 1841. Her obituary stated that she was the oldest Baton Rouge resident at her death. She lived a simple life, never having visited New Orleans nor traveled by train or automobile. Her plain tombstone, though broken, is still readable.

ELIZABETH CHAMBERS
1863 — 1951

Elizabeth "Lizzie" Chambers (1863–1951) and her sister Maud (1876–1960) were the aunts of noted Louisiana writer Lyle Chambers Saxon. Both were graduates of New Orleans Charity Hospital nursing school. Elizabeth was in one of the first graduating classes. To the left of Lyle's grave is the grave of his mother, Katherine "Kitty" Saxon (1868–1915), and to his right is his aunt Maude. On the far side of Katherine lies her aunt Elizabeth.

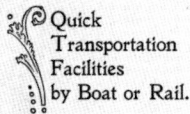

The 1907 *Elks Souvenir of Baton Rouge* contains "an historic, commercial and industrial review of prominent advantages of the parish of East Baton Rouge and the flower city of Louisiana. Dedicated to the Benevolent and Protective Order of Elks, Lodge No. 490." It was edited and published by E.M. Muse whose company also provided the artwork. The advertising pages in the *Elks Souvenir of Baton Rouge* detail the history of Baton Rouge and the lives and deaths of its citizens, as do the tombstone inscriptions in Magnolia Cemetery. For example, members of the Chambers family were druggists, as shown here, and members of the Jolly family were dentists. Other advertisers on this page have family members buried in Magnolia Cemetery, such as those of the Fuqua, Goodwin, and LeBlanc families. (Courtesy of the East Baton Rouge Parish Library.)

Lyle Chambers Saxon (1891–1946) grew up in Baton Rouge, and he and his mother, Katherine Saxon, are interred near her sisters Lizzie and Maud Chambers in Section No. 1, Lot No. 86. Both his mother and paternal grandmother were journalists, and Saxon became a journalist after attending Louisiana State University. His maternal grandfather, Michael Chambers (1838–1931), owned the first bookstore established in Baton Rouge and is buried nearby. Lyle Saxon is credited with saving and bringing to print many Louisiana folktales. In 1935, Saxon became the state director of the Federal Writers' Project in Louisiana and wrote several books still popular with readers of Louisiana-themed books. Before the 30th anniversary of Saxon's 1946 death, friends and admirers erected a new tombstone for him and held a rededication ceremony at his grave. (Both, courtesy of the State Library of Louisiana.)

Lyle Chambers Saxon died in his adopted home of New Orleans, and after a ceremony there, he was returned to Baton Rouge for services at St. James Episcopal Church and burial in Magnolia Cemetery. His tombstone reads: "For this honorable man we pay not our / last respects, but offer instead, everlasting / homage for his noble spirit which so / enriched all our lives. / Author-Writer-Philosopher." (Courtesy of the State Library of Louisiana.)

Tennessee native John William Bates (1837–1909) was a captain in Company H, Mississippi Infantry, and was the sheriff of East Baton Rouge Parish from 1878 to 1888. Bates was a founder and officer in the Baton Rouge Confederate Veterans Association. His spouse, Lucy Hackett Bates (1848–1913), and he had eight children, and they are all buried in Magnolia Cemetery as well.

Edward White Robertson (1823–1887), Section No. 1, Lot No. 92, was a captain in the 27th Louisiana Infantry during the Civil War and served in the Mexican-American War in 1846. Robinson was elected a state representative in 1847–1849 and 1853; he served as the state auditor from 1857 to 1862 and was elected to the US House of Representatives and served from 1877 to 1883. Elected to Congress again in 1886, he died before the term began.

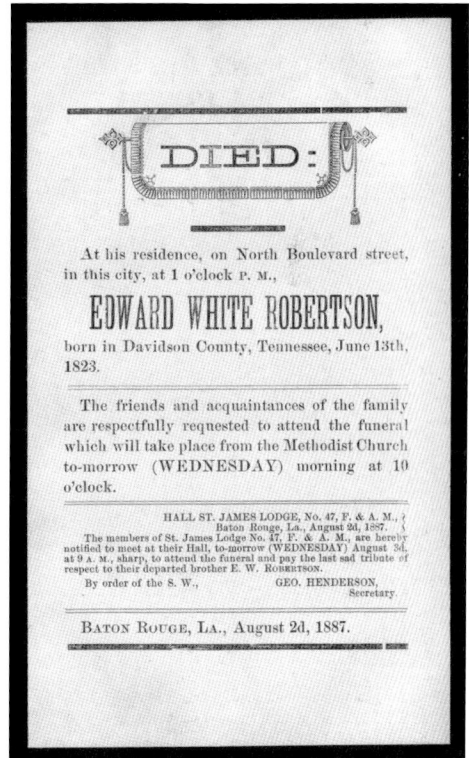

Edward White Robertson's funeral notice identifies his residence as being on North Boulevard and encourages fellow members of the St. James Lodge No. 47, Free and Accepted Masons, to attend his funeral at the Methodist church. (Courtesy of Baton Rouge Funeral Notices, Louisiana and Lower Mississippi Valley Collections, LSU Libraries.)

Samuel Matthews Robertson (1852–1912) was elected to Congress to fill the vacancy caused by the death of his father, Edward, in 1887 and was reelected for eight terms, serving from 1887 to 1907. He returned to Baton Rouge to practice law, and from 1908 to 1911 served as the superintendent of the Louisiana School for the Deaf and Dumb. Robertson's memorial is a Woodmen of the World rough-hewn pillar.

Before his election to Congress, Samuel M. Robertson had served in the Louisiana House of Representatives in 1879 and as a faculty member at Louisiana State University in 1880. As a young man, he attended Magruder's Collegiate Institute in Baton Rouge and studied law at LSU, graduating in 1874. (Courtesy of the State Library of Louisiana.)

Two

A Good Life Hath But Few Days

Located in Section No. 2, Lot No. 11, the full epitaph of John McCartney Taylor (1830–1867) reads, "A good life hath but few days / but a good name endureth forever." Taylor became the assistant editor of the *Daily Advocate* in 1854, and later editor and owner. He served as a Louisiana state senator. Taylor fought for the Confederate States of America at the 1862 Battle of Baton Rouge, and later was severely wounded near Chattanooga, Tennessee.

An obelisk for John McCartney Taylor stands flanked by smaller tombstones for his wife, Eliza Ann Montan Taylor (1837–1887), and son Willard "Little Toomie" Montan Taylor, who died on October 9, 1858, at 11 months old. The single broken rose on Little Toomie's gravestone symbolized his sad death. Nearby is Tonie Harriet Montan, perhaps a cousin, who died at 10 months old in 1859.

In Section No. 2, Lot No. 1, is the cenotaph (a monument without a grave beneath it) erected for Thomas Withers Chinn (1791–1852). He supported the establishment of Magnolia Cemetery and wanted to be buried there; however, he is buried near Rosedale, Louisiana. His wife, Elizabeth Johnson (1794–1877); daughter Mary Jane Robertson (1821–1867); and granddaughters Elizabeth Chinn (1851–1908), Frederica Conrad Chinn (1858–1889), and Frances Conrad Robertson (1860–1930) rest in the memorial vault.

William James Knox (1847–1919) was the founder of the Baton Rouge Bank and a successful businessman. This is the only surviving photograph of his grave taken on the day of his burial. He is buried next to his wife, Robertine Green Knox (1885–1908). Their son King Harding Knox (1878–1951) and his wife, Juliet Dunbar Knox (1883–1965), are also buried in Magnolia. (Courtesy of Larry Gates.)

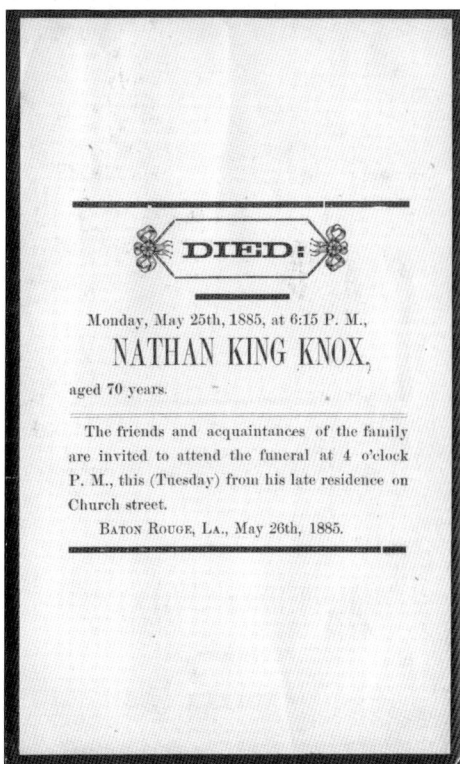

DIED:

Monday, May 25th, 1885, at 6:15 P. M.,

NATHAN KING KNOX,

aged 70 years.

The friends and acquaintances of the family are invited to attend the funeral at 4 o'clock P. M., this (Tuesday) from his late residence on Church street.

BATON ROUGE, LA., May 26th, 1885.

Nathan King Knox (1814–1885) was the father of William James Knox. At the time of his death, he and his family lived on Church Street. Buried nearby are sons William and Nathan King Knox (1852–1909), daughter Ella Knox Keener (1850–1935), and wife, Zipporah Bryan Knox (1826–1886). (Courtesy of Baton Rouge Funeral Notices, Louisiana and Lower Mississippi Valley Collections, LSU Libraries.)

From the Buchel monument, a wide view of Section No. 2 shows the variety of tombstones and monuments that can be seen throughout Magnolia Cemetery. Michael Buchel (1812–1865) and his wife, Margaretha Pfeifer Buchel (1821–1907), Lot No. 85, have an unusual grave monument. The arched gate symbolizes the door to heaven, and each column of the gate is engraved, one with the word "mother" and the other with the word "father." Below their names, it reads "At rest." Their home was on Gracie Street near Decatur Street, and Margaretha's funeral was held there. At the time of her passing, announcements of deaths were known as funeral tickets. Many were printed by the local newspaper office and then posted around town the day after a person's death to give funeral details. Also buried here are descendants Mena Buchel (1854–1935) and Selina L. Buchel (1865–1940).

Titled "Asleep," this death notice for Margaretha informs the reader that she was a native of Germany, lived on Gracie Street, and was to be interred in Magnolia Cemetery on February 26, 1907. Her husband, Michael, was born in Baden, Germany. (Courtesy of the Saucier Family Papers, Louisiana and Lower Mississippi Valley Collections, LSU Libraries.)

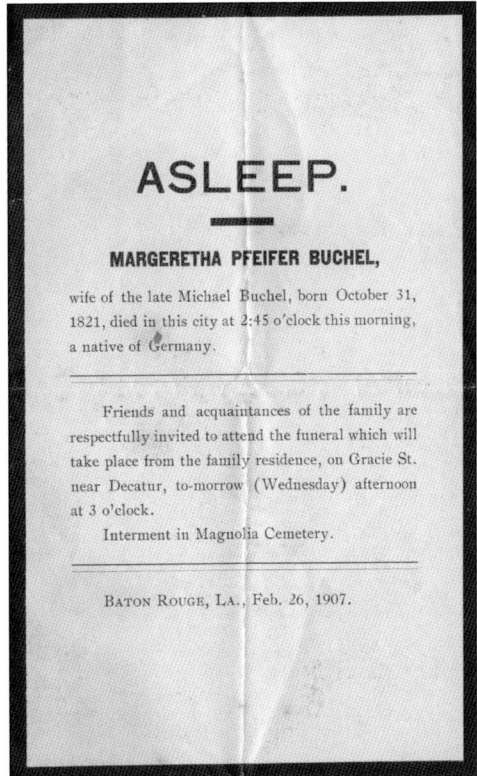

ASLEEP.

MARGERETHA PFEIFER BUCHEL,

wife of the late Michael Buchel, born October 31, 1821, died in this city at 2:45 o'clock this morning, a native of Germany.

Friends and acquaintances of the family are respectfully invited to attend the funeral which will take place from the family residence, on Gracie St. near Decatur, to-morrow (Wednesday) afternoon at 3 o'clock.

Interment in Magnolia Cemetery.

BATON ROUGE, LA., Feb. 26, 1907.

James Mason Elam married Rebecca Chambers (1803–1853) in 1820, and they had 11 children. Their son James Essex Elam (1829–1873) was elected mayor of Baton Rouge four times. Mayor Elam and his wife, Mary S. Vanlandingham Elam (1838–1918), and many family members are buried in the Elam family plot in Section No. 2, Lot No. 98.

Near the Elam plot, the obelisk of R. Durbin Day (1837–1869) is topped by an unfurling scroll, symbolizing death and the hope of resurrection. "My Husband" is written on the scroll. The monument of his wife, Florida C. Elam Day (1843–1874), reads, "Sacred / to the memory / of / Florida," and celebrates her name in a wreath of flowers held up by ribbons and doves, signifying God's love. A short obelisk is dedicated to the "Only children / of / R.D. & F.C. Day": Lillie Elam Day (1863–1865), Edward Durbin Day (1861–1863), and infant son (born and died April 5, 1866). One can track the intermarriage of many families with the help of tombstone inscriptions at Magnolia Cemetery. The Day family intermarried with the Elam family, and the Elam family intermarried with the Chambers family. Florida Elam Day was a sister of James Essex Elam, who became a mayor of Baton Rouge.

James Mason Elam (1796–1856) was a native of Virginia and a veteran of the War of 1812. As an ensign aboard the USS *Guerriere* in 1815, he participated in an attack on the Barbary pirates off the coast of Algeria. In 1820, Elam moved to Baton Rouge and became a lawyer. He ran unsuccessfully for the US House of Representatives in the Third District of Louisiana in 1843. (Courtesy of the East Baton Rouge Parish Library.)

James H. Hallett, representative of Stone and Webster, owners of the Baton Rouge Electric Light and Gas Company, inspects work on the extension of the Baton Rouge Streetcar line on Dufrocq Street, now Nineteenth Street, in 1907. Visible in the background is the iron fence surrounding Magnolia Cemetery. Homes of the era are seen opposite the fence. (Courtesy of the East Baton Rouge Parish Library.)

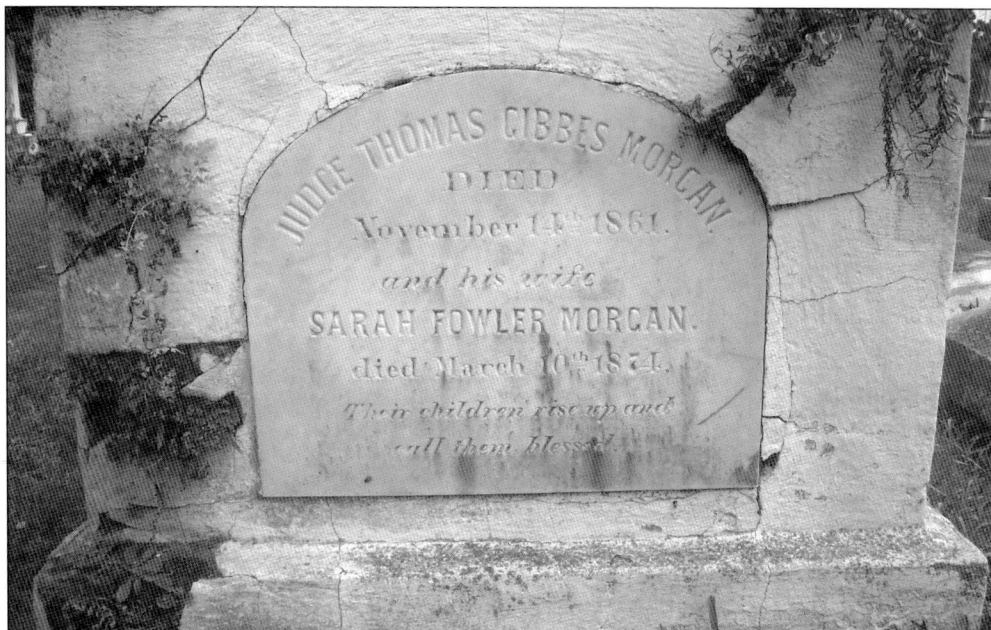

Thomas Gibbs Morgan (1799–1861) and his wife, Sarah Hunt Fowler (1807–1874), are buried together in Section No. 2, Lot No. 39. He was a lawyer, judge, and tax collector in New Orleans. Capt. Thomas Morgan Jr. (1835–1864) and Dr. Henry Waller Fowler Morgan (1836–1861), two of their sons, are also buried in Magnolia. The published diary of their daughter Sarah Morgan Dawson (1842–1909) details the Federal occupation of Baton Rouge during the Civil War. She is buried in Paris, France.

Photographer and Ohio native Andrew David Lytle (1834–1917), Section No. 2, Lot No. 88, arrived in Baton Rouge around 1858. In 1901, Lytle served as the secretary of the Magnolia Cemetery board. Buried with him are his wife, Mary Ann Lunde (1836–1898), and their sons Andrew (1857–1859), William (1862–1868), and Howard (1870–1915). The only child to survive him was Ethel Lytle Hearin (1871–1951), who is buried in her husband's family lot in Magnolia.

Folklore credits Lytle with being a spy for the Confederacy by taking photographs of Union encampments during the occupation of Baton Rouge and having the photographs delivered to Southern leaders. If he was a spy, he was not a clandestine one, for he could not have hidden his large, heavy camera and other equipment from the vantage points where his photographs of the Union forces were made. Lytle began his Baton Rouge photographic studio in 1857. He and his son Howard Lytle advertised their company and photography services in the 1907 *Elks Souvenir of Baton Rouge*. Other advertisers, one local, the Ben R. Mayer Grocery Company, and one regional, the W.W. Homes Company, appear on the same page. Andrew and Howard took the photographs for the *Elks Souvenir of Baton Rouge*. (Courtesy of the East Baton Rouge Parish Library.)

IN MEMORY OF
C. F. RABENHORST.
A NATIVE OF PRUSSIA
GERMANY.
DIED
OCTOBER 4TH 1880.
AGED 52 YRS 2 MO 21 DYS.
May his soul rest in peace.
Capt. 20th La. Inft. C.S.A.

Prussian Charles Ferdinand Rabenhorst (1828–1880), Section No. 2, Lot No. 50, came to Baton Rouge to establish a cabinetmaking business. He was a captain in Company C, 20th Louisiana Infantry. In 1866, he founded the Rabenhorst Funeral Parlor. Today, the Rabenhorst Funeral Homes & Crematory is the oldest continuously operating family business in the city. He and Caroline T. Focken Rabenhorst (1835–1894) met around the time they arrived in New Orleans.

The Rabenhorst plot next to Charles and Caroline is that of Alvina Caroline Rabenhorst (1854–1899), nicknamed "Miss Beanie." Her home was located on Florida Street in the rear of the Istrouma Hotel. Her 1890 portrait was taken at the Lytle Studio. Miss Beanie's tombstone is very similar to those of Charles and Caroline, as well as the tombstone of Ida. (Courtesy of Karen Rabenhorst Kerr.)

Ida Wilhemena Rabenhorst (1868–1895) married Joseph Richard Barillier (1866–1922), and her sister Caroline "Carrie" (1864–1961) married William Tell Barillier (1864–1952). Several members of the Barillier family worked for the Rabenhorst Funeral Home. Ida's portrait was taken in Baton Rouge by the Owen brothers, traveling photographers. (Courtesy of Karen Rabenhorst Kerr.)

Owen Bros.   *Traveling Photographers.*

For the 100th anniversary of the death of Charles Ferdinand Rabenhorst (1828–1880), members of the family gathered at his grave in Magnolia Cemetery. Pictured are the current and fourth-generation operators of the Rabenhorst funeral business. Two young sons, Ferdinand H. (1861–1865) and Charles W. (1872–1873), are also buried in the plot. (Courtesy of Karen Rabenhorst Kerr.)

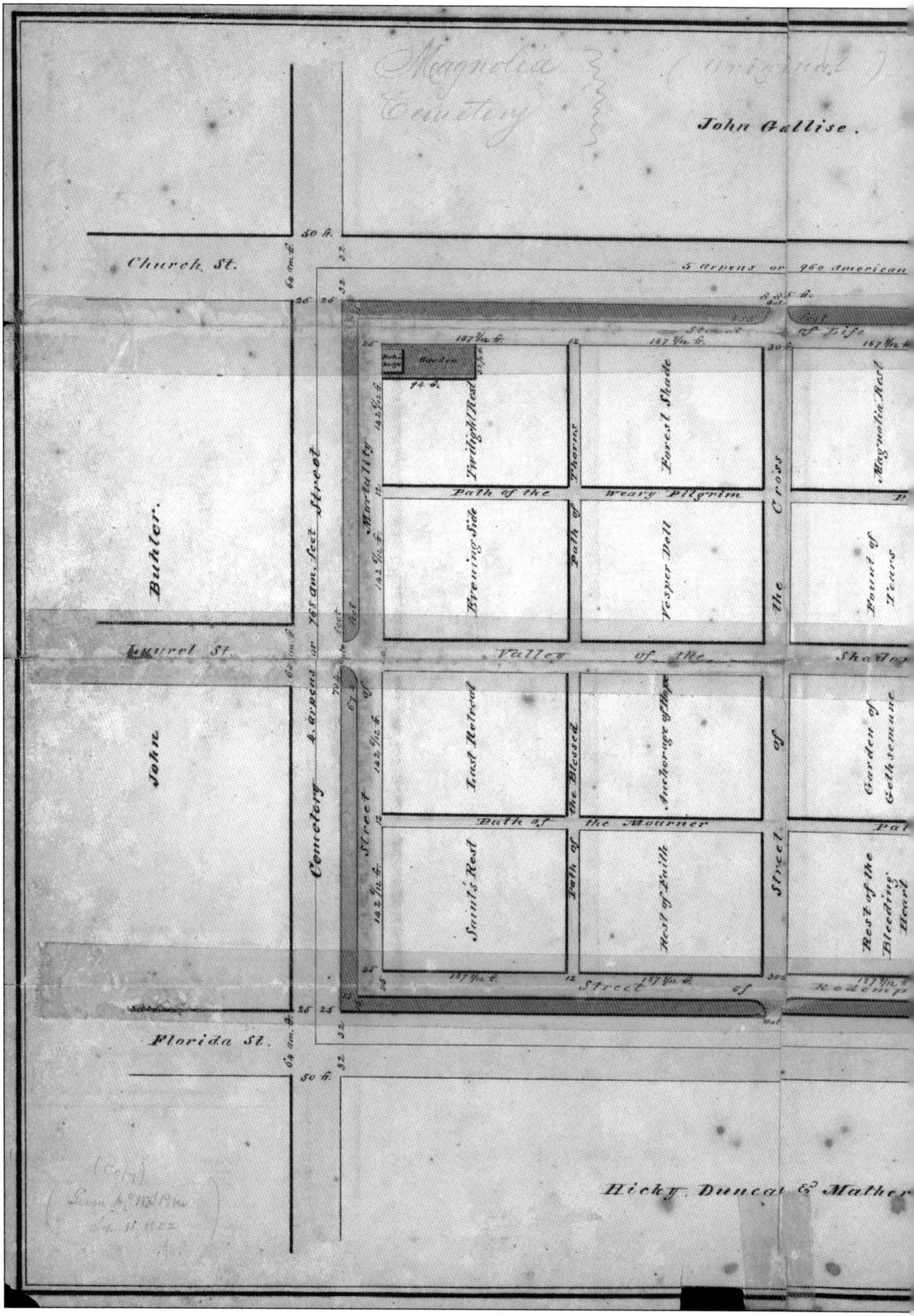

Magnolia Cemetery (original)

John Gallise.

Church St.

50 ft.

5 arpens or 960 american

Butler.

Cemetery   4 Arpens or 760 am. feet Street

Laurel St.

John.

Florida St.

Garden

Mortality

Twilight Rest   Path of the   Forest Shade   Magnolia Rest

Evening Side   Path of the   Vesper Dell   Weary Pilgrim   the Cross   Fount of Tears

Valley   of   the   Shades

Last Retreat   Anchorage of Hope   of   Garden of Gethsemane

Saints Rest   Path of the   Host of Faith   the Mourner   Street   Rest of the Bleeding Heart

Street   of   Redemp

Hicky, Duncan & Mather

42

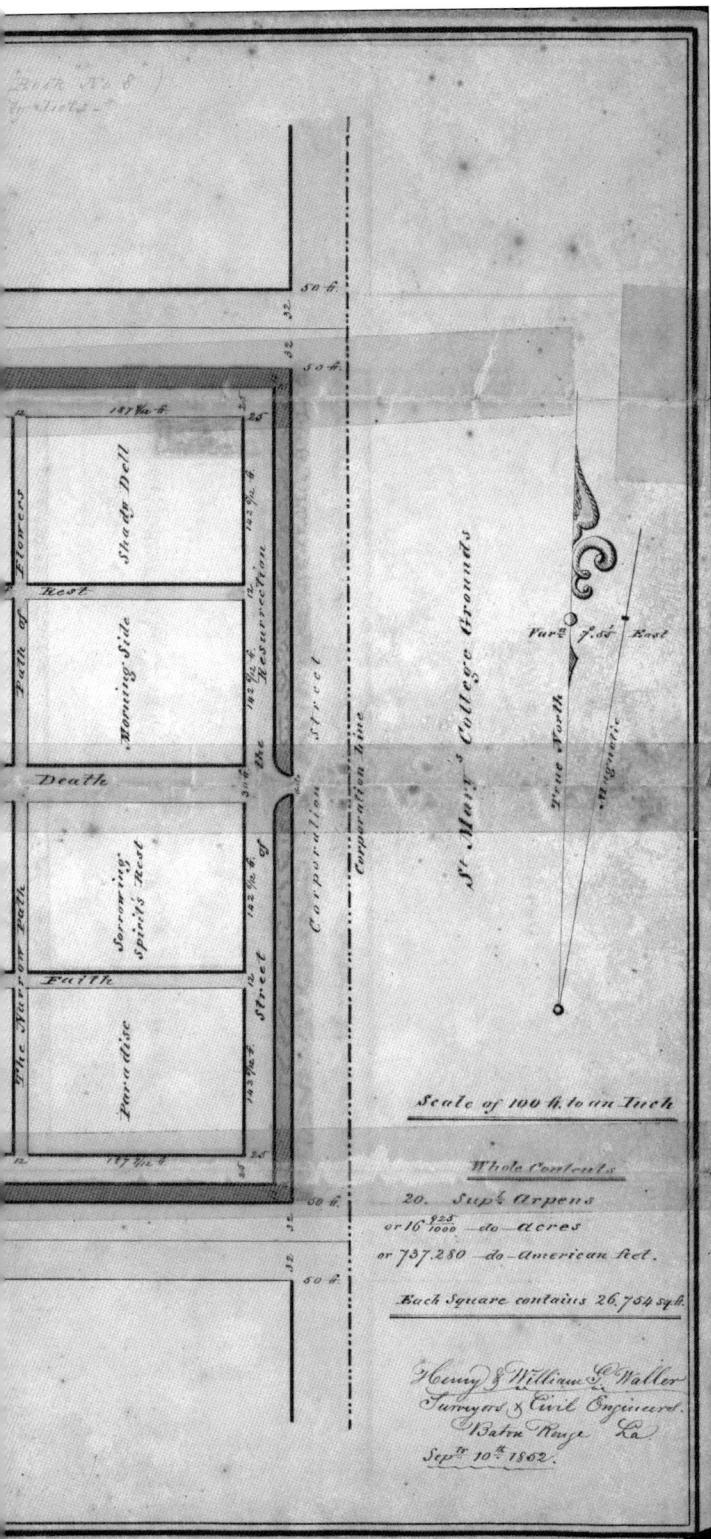

Map labels (as visible on the survey):

- Shady Dell
- Rest
- Morning Side
- Death
- Sorrowing Spirits Rest
- Faith
- Paradise
- Path of Flowers
- The Narrow Path
- The Resurrection
- Corporation Street
- Corporation Line
- St. Mary's College Grounds
- True North
- Magnetic
- Var⁴ 7.55 East

Scale of 100 ft. to an Inch

Whole Contents
20. Sup⁴ Arpens
or 16 925/1000 do — Acres
or 737.280 do — American Act.

Each Square contains 26,754 sq.ft.

Henry & William G. Waller
Surveyors & Civil Engineers.
Baton Rouge La
Sep⁴ 10ᵗʰ 1852.

William G. Waller and Company provided property surveys for individuals, businesses, and government offices in East Baton Rouge Parish. William G. Waller (1813–1891), a native of New York, is buried in Magnolia Cemetery. His 1852 map of the planned cemetery proposed names for the lanes and the burial sections. The surveyor was lyrical in his choices, writing on the survey the Street of Mortality, the Street of the Cross, the Street of the Resurrection, and the Path of the Blessed, among others. For the burial sections, some of his suggestions were Saints' Rest, Forest Shade, Vesper Dell, Fount of Tears, and Morning Side. None of his names were used, but the cemetery retains Waller's proposed layout. (Courtesy of the William G. Waller Collection, Louisiana and Lower Mississippi Valley Collections, LSU Libraries.)

The tombstone of Mary M. Denham Piper (1826–1892) states that she was the "Daughter of Giseilia & William Denham / Wife of Jacob Piper." While her tombstone is still standing, her husband's is on the ground. The graves near Mary and Jacob (died 1875) tell a story of loss and heartbreak for five of their children, Frances Hannah (1853–1864), Mary Tunnard (1851–1859), George Enochs (February to June 1870), infant son (born and died October 9, 1868), and another infant son (died October 26, 1867, 21 days). Only one son, Willie H. Piper (1855–1883), lived to adulthood. One stone represents the three infants and perhaps originally had carved lambs or something similar on top. The fence shows evidence of neglect. A fence corner post shows more clearly the tree motif with limbs cut away to represent the end of life; however, ivy adorns the fence, which symbolizes resurrection.

The unique gravesite of Robert George Beale (1823–1859) has a sarcophagus and a tombstone with an open, shield-like scroll showing the following epitaph: "Sacred to the / memory of / Robert George Beale." It ends with "He trusted in God." Nearby are Anne Maria Beale (1853–1933); Augusta Saunders King Beale (1857–1919) and her husband, Lindsay Dunn Beale (1856–1923); Jennie Munson Beale (1889–1957); and Thomas Buffington Beale (1888–1959).

Few photographs of Beale family members still exist. Anne Maria Beale, known as Annie, served as a librarian at Louisiana State University for many years. Faculty photographs, taken in 1916, include this one of Annie. Although the relationships are unclear, Annie and Lindsay may have been the children of Robert George Beale (1823–1859). (Courtesy of LSU Photograph Collection, 1886–1926, Louisiana State University Archives, LSU Libraries.)

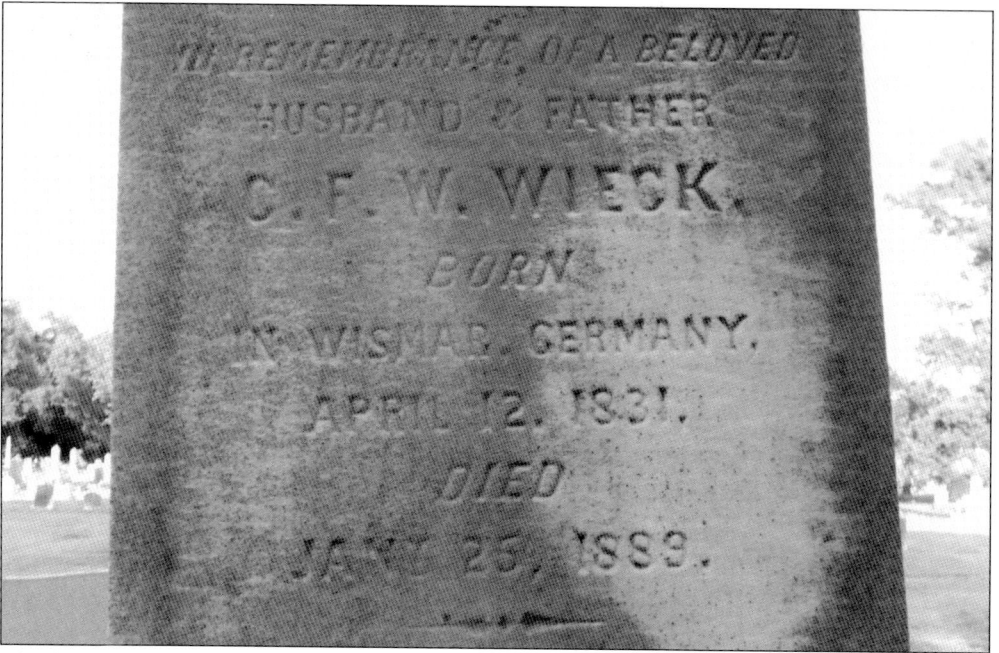

Charles F.W. Wieck (1831–1889) purchased the Rainbow House Saloon in 1861. After Confederate forces fired on Fort Sumter in Charleston, South Carolina, Wieck renamed his business Fort Sumter Saloon and embedded a cannon barrel in the sidewalk. When an effort was made to remove the cannon in the 1960s, citizens stopped it, and it remains at the corner of Third and Laurel Streets.

Eleanor McMain (1866–1934) served as head of the Kingsley House–Home for Girls in New Orleans for 33 years and gained the moniker of "Jane Addams of New Orleans" for her charitable work and as a leader for child labor reform legislation. She died at Kingsley House but is buried in Magnolia next to her father, John Wesley McMain (died 1888), and mother, Jane Walsh McMain (1831–1904).

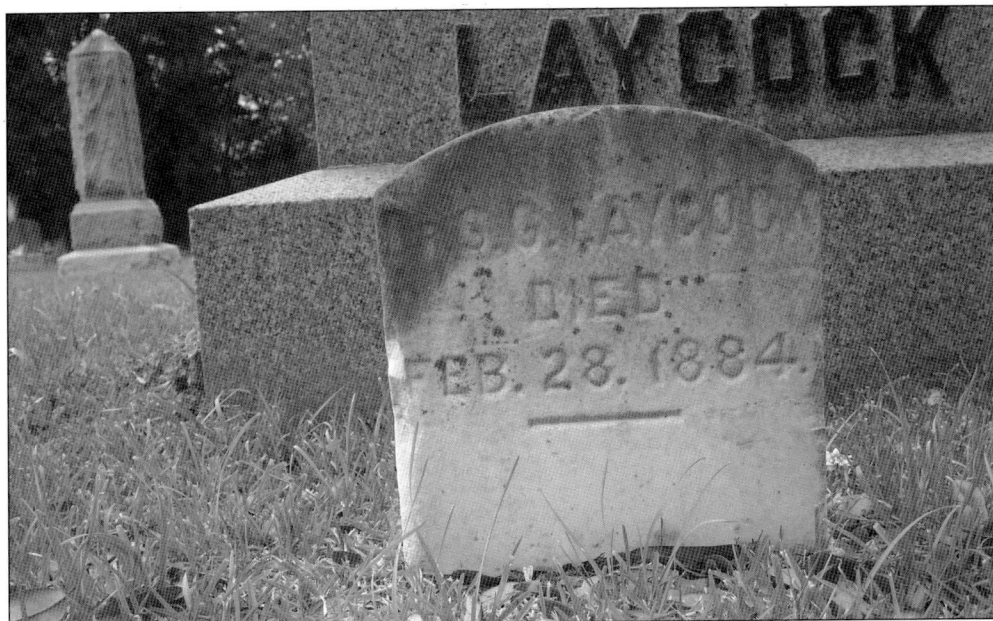

Dr. Samuel G. Laycock (1817–1884) was an Ohio native. Originally, the Laycock family was interred on his plantation, named Goodwood, where he had built an elaborate Greek Revival–style home for his bride. In 1848, Dr. Laycock married Adelia Louise Bird (1829–1865), whose family was prominent in Baton Rouge. After the sale of Goodwood Plantation, Laycock's grave was moved to the Bird family plot in Magnolia.

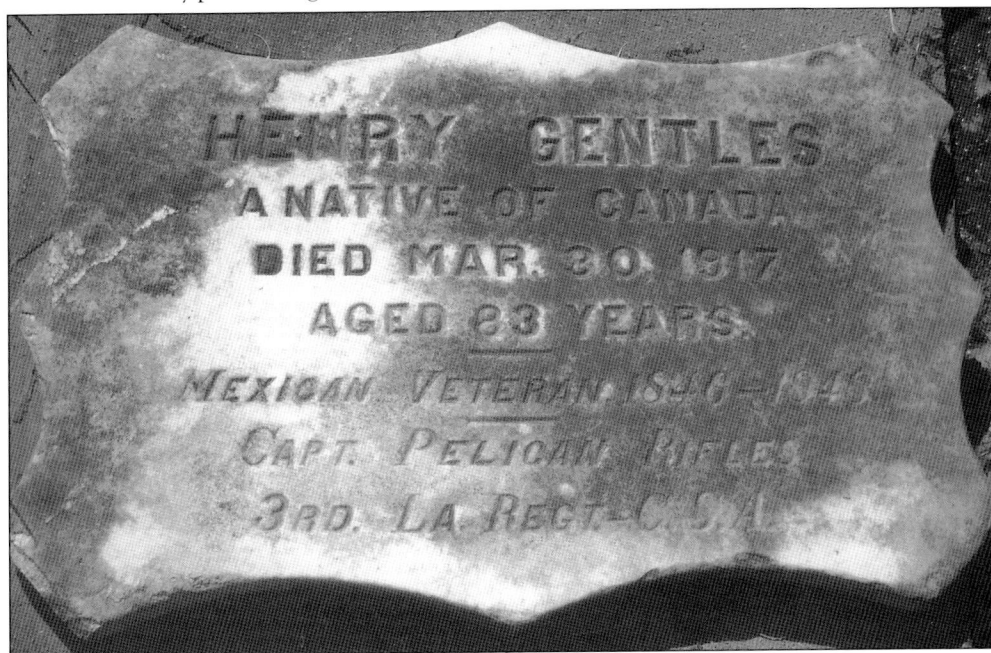

Henry Gentles (1834–1917) served as a captain of the Pelican Rifles, Company K, 3rd Louisiana Regiment, during the Civil War. He was also a veteran of the Mexican-American War, 1846–1848. During the Civil War, he was taken prisoner three separate times. Gentles owned the North Street Brickyard, located near where he and his wife, Kate Collins Gentles (1850–1931), lived.

Looking toward Baton Rouge National Cemetery outside Magnolia Cemetery's fence facing Florida Boulevard and under the 20th-century street pavement lies the mass grave of some of the victims of the 1878 yellow fever epidemic. Approximately 114 victims are buried here. An angel standing beside a thick, plain, obelisk sadly looks down and brings flowers to the lost. In 1852, Magnolia Cemetery extended up to the edge of the original wagon lane that would eventually become Florida Boulevard. As people died, fear of the disease forced the city to quickly bury the deceased in the unused area of the cemetery at the lane. Gradually, the transportation needs of the town led to a widening of the road and, finally, to a full two-lane gravel road named Florida Boulevard. It was paved around 1930. Three young children in the well-known Jolly family, Emmett, Charles, and Lawrence, died in the 1878 epidemic.

LEST WE FORGET
THE YELLOW FEVER EPIDEMIC OF 1878
OVER 100 VICTIMS LAID TO REST IN HISTORIC MAGNOLIA CEMETERY

In 2008, the Foundation for Historical Louisiana (renamed Preserve Louisiana) erected this monument in remembrance of those long forgotten. Most of the adults and children died between August 18 and November 18, 1878. In early September, the New Orleans *Morning Star and Catholic Messenger* newspaper reported that, while Baton Rouge had 163 known cases of yellow fever, only 15 people had died. The epidemic unfortunately spread quickly, and by the middle of September, an average of 40 new cases appeared each day. By the end of November, over 100 had died in Baton Rouge. Quarantines were enforced by armed guards at the port and roads leading into Baton Rouge. A listing of the names of some of those who died in Baton Rouge appeared in the *Baton Rouge Weekly Advocate* on November 22, 1878. The 1878 yellow fever epidemic caused over 20,000 deaths throughout the entire Lower Mississippi River region.

William Hezekiah Nathaniel Magruder (1815–1900), Section No. 2, Lot No. 18, was the founder of Magruder's Collegiate Institute in 1855 for higher education of young men in the area. Magruder closed the institute in 1888 after Louisiana State University came to Baton Rouge. He served as the superintendent of the State Institution for the Blind from 1889 to 1900. He is buried next to his wife, Mary Bangs Magruder (1818–1899).

Interred in Section No. 2, Lot No. 76, Maj. David French Boyd (1834–1899), 9th Louisiana Infantry, and brother Thomas Duckett Boyd both served as presidents of LSU. David was president in 1877 when the school officially became Louisiana State University and Agricultural and Mechanical College, the federally mandated land grant college of Louisiana. Ester Gertrude Wright (1844–1915) married Boyd in 1865. They had eight children, one of whom, Leroy (1873–1936), is buried with them.

Oliver Perry Smith (1839–1927) was a captain in Company C, 2nd Louisiana Regiment. Smith's tombstone bears the outline of the Southern Cross of Honor. Shown is another stone for Smith, which may have been the first headstone on his grave. His family moved from Alabama to Louisiana when he was one year old. Five of his seven brothers also joined Confederate military units, and all survived the war. After the Civil War, Oliver and his brother Claiborne worked in business as dry goods salesmen in Union Parish. In 1887, Oliver accepted a position in the office of the state auditor. He married Frances Elizabeth Goldsby (1847–1885), and they had three daughters. Although wounded on August 20, 1862, at the Second Battle of Manassas, Captain Smith lived to be 87 years old.

Often, damage to tombstones and grave markers is not repaired because there are no descendants to care for the plots. The Dunn family plot is one of these. The parts of the broken obelisk from the tombstone of Eliza Alexina Dunn Buffington (1829–1871) lie atop the sarcophagus of another Dunn family member. She was the oldest daughter of Alex M. Dunn (1805–?) and Eliza L. Dunn. Her husband, Thomas J. Buffington (1821–1903), was a well-known medical doctor and surgeon during the Civil War and later in Louisiana and Mississippi. Dr. Buffington is buried in St. Joseph's Cemetery. To the right is the grave and obelisk of her mother, Eliza L. Dunn (1803–1861), and next to Eliza is Lindsay Coleman Dunn (1835–1855), the only son of A.M. & E.L. Dunn. The Buffingtons had no children. The Dunn, Buffington, and Beale families were related by marriage.

Three

FURTHER DEVELOPMENT OF GOD'S KINGDOM

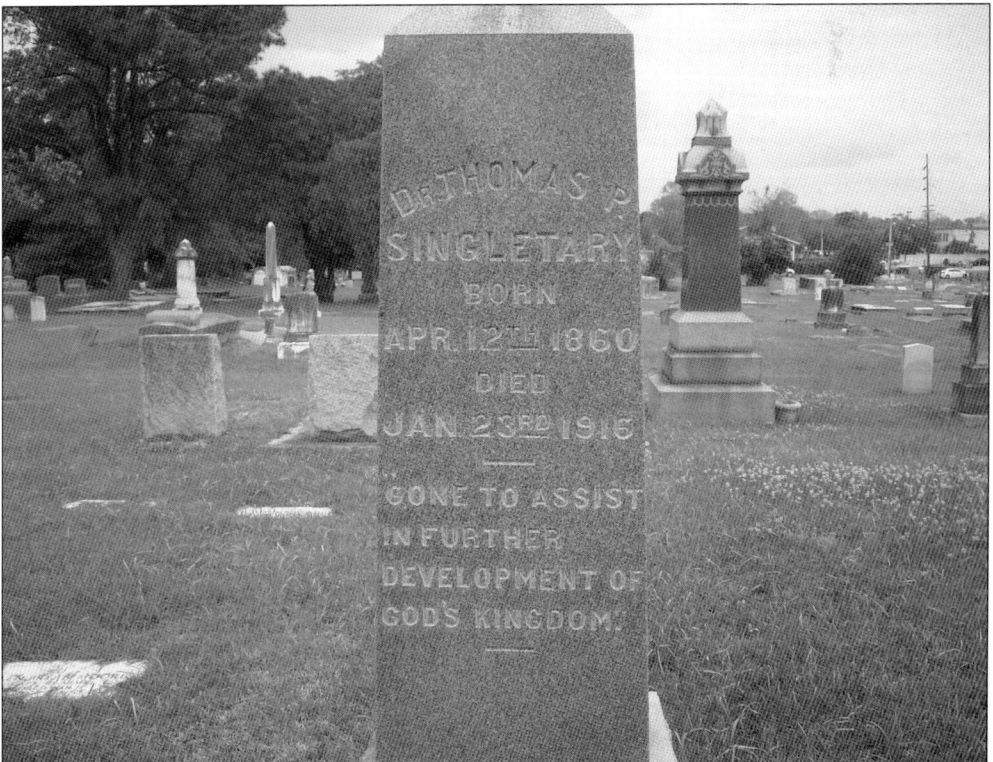

Located in Section No. 3, Lot No. 70, the epitaph on the tombstone of Dr. Thomas Puller Singletary (1860–1916) reads, "Gone to assist / in the further / development of / God's Kingdom." He served the Baton Rouge community as the East Baton Rouge Parish coroner and founded the Baton Rouge Sanitarium. Singletary's traditional Egyptian-style obelisk represents a ray of sunlight, which connects heaven and earth.

A crypt near the Wax family graves in Section No. 3, Lot No. 7, has gained an unwelcome roof garden of weeds. Magnolia Cemetery does not have perpetual care, so descendants are responsible for maintaining the graves. Nearby are Ruemelli Willie Wax (1895–1918), Edward Wax Sr. (1857–1937), Sophie Wieck Wax (1857–1935), Nicholas Vaughn Wax (1907–1908), Charles Nicholas Wax (June–September 1881), and Louise Wax Landry (1882–1935), daughter of Edward and Sophie.

William Brainerd Spencer (1835–1882), Section No. 3, Lot No. 30, graduated in 1857 from the law department of the University of Louisiana in New Orleans. Spencer was elected to the 44th US Congress and served from 1876 to 1877. He resigned to accept the appointment as an associate justice of the Louisiana Supreme Court, serving until 1880. He died in 1882 at Jalapa, Mexico. He and Henrietta Elam Spencer (1838–1888) had five children.

Thomas Sambola Jones (1859–1933), Section No. 3, Lot No. 30, was an educator, attorney, and a newspaper owner and editor; served in the Louisiana House of Representatives; and was a city court judge in East Baton Rouge Parish. He was the US minister to Honduras from 1918 to 1921. Jones married Deborah Henrietta Spencer (1858–1889), daughter of W.B. Spencer, and they had one child, Eliza Perry Jones Halligan (1887–1916). (Courtesy of the Library of Congress.)

Capt. Edward A. Yorke (1813–1892), Section No. 3, Lot No. 47, became the owner of Moss Side Plantation near Baton Rouge around 1880. He was a sailor and ship captain for the US Lighthouse Establishment based out of Philadelphia until 1863, when he moved to New Orleans. He also oversaw lighthouse construction in the Florida Keys. Yorke married twice, and both wives are buried in New Orleans.

Henry Luse Fuqua (1865–1926) was elected Louisiana's 39th governor in 1924 and died in office. He operated Fuqua Hardware Company in Baton Rouge for nearly 40 years and served as warden of the Louisiana State Penitentiary at Angola from 1916 until 1924. After his funeral at St. James Episcopal Church, the large group of mourners followed the hearse on foot as it drove away to Magnolia Cemetery. Later, he and other Fuqua family members were moved to Roselawn Memorial Park. His wife, Marie Laure Matta Fuqua (1866–1968), lived to be 102 years old. Sons James Overton Fuqua (1893–1900) and Henry Luse Fuqua Jr. (1905–1992) are buried with their parents. (Both, courtesy of the East Baton Rouge Parish Library.)

An area known as the Confederate burial pit, Section No. 3, Lots Nos. 80–82, was purported to be the final location of Confederate soldiers killed in the August 1862 battle. Some of the heaviest fighting took place in and near the cemetery. Grave markers, trees, and the cemetery's picket fence were used as cover by both Confederate and Union troops.

Some Confederate veterans' headstones are arranged around the perimeter of the pit, but the actual graves may be elsewhere because tombstones have been moved, damaged, and lost since the first burials. Henry Turner (?–1862), a private in Company B, 9th Battery, Louisiana Infantry, was killed in the Battle of Baton Rouge. His gravestone bears the outline of the Southern Cross of Honor.

The United Confederate Veterans Association purchased this site around 1896. It is believed the memorial was erected in the 1930s by the Joanna Waddill Chapter of the United Daughters of the Confederacy. Local lore holds that most of the Confederate soldiers killed that day were buried in a common burial pit in Section No. 3. Like Turner, many soldiers have individual tombstones, but many have been moved, and original interment sites are unknown. Such tombstones probably are not over anyone's remains. An archeological investigation by Coastal Environments Inc. in 1992 suggests that there were no burials in the pit area. The research was prepared for the Division of Archaeology, Louisiana Department of Culture, Recreation & Tourism, and the Foundation for Historical Louisiana. Many Confederate veterans who died after August 1862 are buried throughout Magnolia Cemetery near family members.

A wider view of the memorial and its plot shows the standing headstones for Confederate veterans as well as flat headstones for others. Most of these markers have the Southern Cross of Honor whether they are upright, such as the one for Henry Turner, or flat markers on the ground, such as the one for Robert Hauge.

ROBERT McEWEN HAGUE
IST LIEUT CO E 9 KY MTD IN
CONFEDERATE STATES ARMY
22 1825   AUG 5 1862

Having enlisted from his home in Lincoln County, Tennessee, Robert McEwen Hague Sr. (1825–1862), Section No. 3, Lot No. 79, went on to become a first lieutenant in Company E, 9th Kentucky Mounted Infantry. His headstone is near the Confederate monument. When he left home, his wife, Cordelia Jane Alexander Hague (1818–1888), was pregnant with their fifth child, born after his father's death in the August 1862 Battle of Baton Rouge. The baby was named Robert McEwen Hague Jr.

Sardinia, Indiana, native Rueben F. Patterson (1834–1908), Section No. 3, Lot No. 79, was commissioned in Company I, 68th Indiana Infantry, and rose to the rank of captain. His wife was Angeline Patterson (1838–?). It is unclear when they moved to Baton Rouge, but in the 1905 Baton Rouge city directory, he is listed as Reverend Patterson.

Born in Amite County, Mississippi, Zachariah Richardson Causey (1822–1862), Section No. 3, Lot No. 79, was a second lieutenant in Company B, 9th Louisiana Infantry. He died in the 1862 Battle of Baton Rouge. Evidently, Causey was buried after the battle, and his body was never claimed by his family for reburial in his Mississippi home. Causey and his wife, Frances "Fannie" Victoria Jones, had 12 children.

Oscar Heady Foreman (1833–1905), Section No. 3, Lot No. 110, was in Company B, 7th Louisiana Infantry, and served as the Baton Rouge police chief from 1874 to 1876. His tombstone shows the Masons' emblem of the compass and level. He and his wife, Thyrza Rowley Foreman (1838–1913), share the same tombstone. A child, Linda F. Foreman (1863–1866), has an inscription on her tombstone in Highland Cemetery reading "Daughter of O.H. & T.A. Foreman."

WILLIAM GARIG.

William W. Garig (1839–1908) served in Company A, 11th Louisiana Infantry, in the Civil War but emerged after the war to become a prominent Baton Rouge businessman. He and Susan B. Freeman Garig (1840–1915) were the parents of Louise, Mercedes, Ned, George, and Ruckins Garig. They are buried near their children in Magnolia Cemetery. (Courtesy of the East Baton Rouge Parish Library.)

Louise Garig (1880–1935) and Mercedes M. Garig (1877–1957) were members of the first class of undergraduate women admitted to Louisiana State University in 1906, and were two of the first women to graduate with master's degrees. They each taught for over 25 years in the LSU English department. Of the many Garig family members interred in Magnolia Cemetery, Louise's gravestone is the only one carved in script letters. Louise died in a Memphis, Tennessee, hospital after surgery needed because of a car accident in Baton Rouge. (Left, courtesy of LSU Photograph Collection, 1886–1926, Louisiana State University Archives, LSU Libraries.)

Mercedes Garig was fondly known as "Miss Mercy." Louise and Mercedes had three brothers, George Gardner Garig (1876–1961), a veteran of the Spanish-American War; William "Ned" W. Garig Jr. (1870–1931); and Ruckins Robroy Garig (1882–1948). Mercedes and George were born on the Garig plantation on the Amite River in Livingston Parish, Louisiana. (Courtesy of LSU Photograph Collection, 1886–1926, Louisiana State University Archives, LSU Libraries.)

DIED:

At the family residence on the Highland Road, at 11 o'clock a. m. March 5th, 1890,

MRS. E. C. DREHR,

a native of East Feliciana parish, aged 43 years and 3 months.

The friends and relatives of the family are requested to attend the funeral from the family residence to-day (Thursday) at 3 o'clock. The interment will take place at Magnolia Cemetery.

Baton Rouge, La., March 6th, 1890.

Although Emily C. Offutt Drehr (1846–1890) lived closer to Highland Cemetery, she was buried in Magnolia. She was originally from East Feliciana Parish and was the wife of Benjamin F. Drehr (1846–1924). They and their three children, as well as other family members, are buried in Section No. 3, Plot No. 38. (Courtesy of Baton Rouge Funeral Notices, Louisiana and Lower Mississippi Valley Collections, LSU Libraries.)

Martha Malvena Gillespie Cooper (1808–1884) was the second wife of Baton Rouge medical doctor John Witherspoon Pettigrew McGimsey (1796–1874). He was born in Burke County, North Carolina. They married in 1830 and had four children, Martha Elizabeth McGimsey Carruth (?–1918), Eudora A., James G., and William Champe McGimsey. Martha's grave is marked with a draped obelisk. The drape symbolizes the end of life. Her obelisk reads, "Sacred / to the memory of / Mrs. M.M.C. McGimsey / consort of the late / Dr. J.W.P. McGimsey." The term "consort" was seldom used in the late 1880s as "wife" became the preferred term in the United States. Dr. McGimsey's tombstone is elaborate and topped by the Masonic emblem. Its epitaph reads, "Blessed are the pure in heart for they shall see God," and includes a lengthy tribute to his life of good works.

This photograph taken just after World War I shows the double monument to Elizine Kinner Barillier (1836–1897) and Louis J. Barillier (1830–1903), along with evidence of neglect. Natives of Switzerland, their tombstones are centered by a common headstone. Some of their sons worked with the Rabenhorst family in their mortuary business, and their families intermarried. (Courtesy of the East Baton Rouge Parish Library.)

Oscar F. Rabenhorst created the first motor-operated hearse in Baton Rouge. He used his skills as a cabinetmaker to build a wooden hearse on the chassis of a 1920s Ford truck. No less elegant than the horse-drawn hearse carriages used previously, the gasoline-powered hearse had windows on both sides so mourners could view the coffin as the hearse passed by. (Courtesy of Karen Rabenhorst Kerr.)

Ellen Bryan Moore (1912–1999), Section No. 3, Lot No. 67, served as a captain during World War II in the US Army, Women's Army Corps (WACs). She worked to change the WACs from an auxiliary unit to a military force within the Army. Moore earned teaching credentials from LSU, and after the war returned to teaching until 1952, when she was elected as the Louisiana register of state lands, serving four years. She was elected again in 1960 and served until 1976. Moore was one of the first women elected to statewide office in Louisiana. Among her many civic contributions was the establishment of the first soup kitchen in Baton Rouge to aid hungry families. (Left, courtesy of the State Library of Louisiana.)

MAJOR BENJAMIN FRANKLIN
BRYAN
JAN. 3, 1832
JULY 1, 1897

Benjamin Franklin Bryan (1832–1897), Section No. 3, Lot No. 67, is remembered as the city's mayor who refused to surrender Baton Rouge to Federal forces in 1862, claiming he did not have the authority to do so. Soon after, he resigned as mayor and joined the Confederate army. Bryan's wife, Rebecca Coleman Dunn (1837–1908), is buried near him. They were the grandparents of Ellen Bryan Moore.

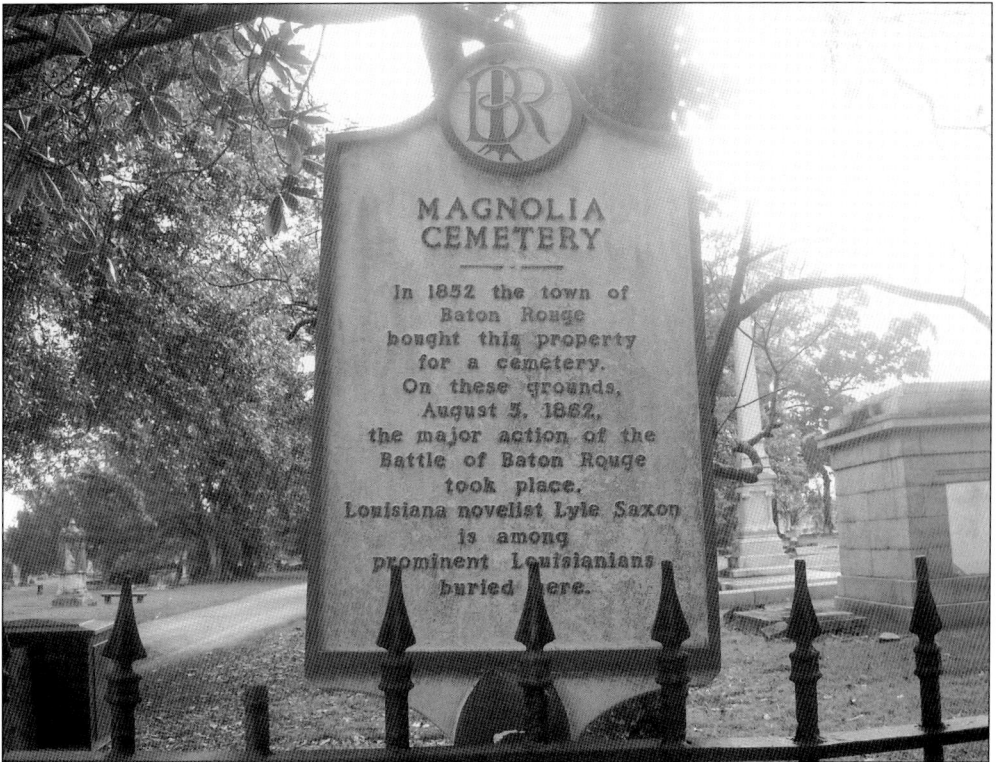

BR

MAGNOLIA
CEMETERY

In 1852 the town of
Baton Rouge
bought this property
for a cemetery.
On these grounds,
August 5, 1862,
the major action of the
Battle of Baton Rouge
took place.
Louisiana novelist Lyle Saxon
is among
prominent Louisianians
buried here.

During the 1976 US bicentennial, Baton Rouge highlighted local historic places throughout town with descriptive markers. The one for Magnolia Cemetery stands near the front entrance close to the Chinn family monument in Section No. 2. When created, the initials "BR" were painted red to signify Baton Rouge's nickname, "Red Stick." A red stick is depicted behind the initials.

The main gate on North Nineteenth Street matches the 1909 cast-iron fence that surrounds the cemetery. The entrance sign is the third that has stood there. The first, erected at an unknown time, was replaced in the 1960s, but the word "Magnolia" was misspelled as "Magnalia." The *a* was removed, and for a few years, the sign read "Magn lia Cemetery."

Magnolia Cemetery was listed in the National Register of Historic Places on January 4, 1985. It was awarded the designation because it not only played an important role in the Civil War's 1862 Battle of Baton Rouge but also has retained its essential appearance and remains in a good state of historical integrity. It is the only part of the battlefield that remains intact because other areas became private property.

Four

A Scholar, a Gentleman, and a Friend

The beautiful, columned mausoleum of Isabel Hill Montan (1852–1877) is adorned with a single rose within an incised diamond on each side panel. Beside her is the grave of her husband, Douglass Cullum Montan (1834–1896); his epitaph, which is elegant in its simplicity, reads "A scholar, a gentleman / and a friend." Her epitaph is "the flower fadeth." Isabel's parents, John Hill (1824–1910) and Catherine McPhail Hill (?–1889), are also buried nearby.

SACRED TO THE ...
... REV ...
DOUGLASS CULLUM MONTAN
BORN IN BATON ROU...
JANUARY 20 ...
DIED IN BATON ROUGE ...
JUNE 9 ...
A SCHOLAR A GENTLEMAN
AND A FRIEND.

Isabel died at her parents' home in West Baton Rouge Parish and was buried in the mausoleum her husband, Douglass Cullum Montan, built for her in Section No. 4, Lot No. 1, adjacent to the Hill family plot. Montan became the editor of the *Advocate*, was president of the Grosse Tête Railroad, and served as the Baton Rouge Parish treasurer, as well as a state senator.

JOSEPH G. ALLEN
SEPT. 6, 1879
OCT. 23 1941

Joseph G. Allen (1879–1941) has a unique tombstone with a flaming oil lamp. Lamps symbolize immortality of the spirit and illumination of the word of God. Allen was a teacher at the Louisiana State School for the Blind in Baton Rouge (previously the Institution for the Blind) and a piano tuner. His wife was Lottie M. Allen (1893–?), and they lived at 346 East Boulevard in 1940.

Throughout Magnolia Cemetery are plots where generations of family members are buried together or in adjacent lots. Like the Montan and Hill families, the LeJeune family members reside together in death. Adam Joseph LeJeune (1870–1947) and Emily McLin LeJeune (1875–1950), Section No. 4, Lot No. 12, both died in traffic accidents just three years apart. Adam was the sexton for Magnolia Cemetery from about 1925 until his death.

Adam and Emily LeJeune's grave markers are a matched set of stone rectangles atop concrete blanket/tablet grave covers, with the name and dates within an incised rectangle and a cross at each top corner. One of their two daughters, Addie LeJeune Meyerer (1901–1969), is also buried in the lot with her parents. Addie's son, William A. Meyerer (1929–2008), is interred nearby.

The tombstone of Deanna Lucertia Morrow Patty (1939–2002) is a large rough-carved stone with an open cross in the center. This is an example of a 21st-century burial in Magnolia. Although she was born in Oklahoma and lived in New Orleans where she died, Patty was buried in Magnolia Cemetery. Her son R. Andrew Patty II lived in Baton Rouge at 353 Nelson Street.

George "Mundy" Mundinger (1854–1910) and his wife, Amelia Henrietta Carstens Mundinger (1854–1920), were both born in New Orleans. Before moving to Harrell's Ferry Road to begin farming, Mundy played baseball for the city league. In May 1884, he tried out for a professional team in Indiana. Around 1905, the family moved to Baton Rouge, and he became involved with local baseball and umpired games at Battle Park.

Samuel McHenry Hart (1816–1898) was the first Baton Rouge fire chief. In 1861, he was one of the wealthiest men in Baton Rouge because of his many business interests. He pushed for commercial buildings to be constructed of brick for fire prevention. Chief Hart was the oldest fireman in the city at the time of his death, and the last living charter member of the Washington Fire Company No. 1.

Robert Andrew Hart (1858–1939), Section No. 4, Lot No. 16, was mayor of Baton Rouge from 1898 to 1902 and was one of the wealthiest men in the city at the time of his death, like his father, Samuel, before him. His mother, Sophie Martin Hart (1821–1907), lies next to him. (Courtesy of the East Baton Rouge Parish Library.)

R. A. HART,
Mayor of Baton Rouge.

ROBERT A. HART.
BORN
OCT. 12TH 1858.
DIED
MAY 25TH 1939.

In 1899, Mayor Hart helped raise funds to build the Convention Street school and the Florida Street school and had parts of North Boulevard, Florida Street, and Convention Street paved. Hart paid for modernizations to the city's infrastructure by issuing bonds. These bonds financed road improvements and paving, the erection of new schools for both black and white students, and the improvement of sewers and drains.

Joseph "Joe" M. Hart (1849–1890), a brother of Mayor Robert A. Hart, died at Hot Springs, Arkansas. His death notice lists groups important in his life: the Knights of Pythias, the Knights of Honor, and the volunteer Pelican Hook and Ladder Fire Company No. 1. (Courtesy of Baton Rouge Funeral Notices, Louisiana and Lower Mississippi Valley Collections, LSU Libraries.)

The Hart family plot is surrounded by a lovely, well-maintained wrought iron fence. Mayor Hart is buried here along with his father, Samuel, and mother, Sophie. The adjacent Lot No. 13 holds some of their nine children, including Margaret Hart Callihan (1846–1898) and her husband, David M. Callihan Jr. (1845–1878), a second lieutenant in Company D, 23rd Tennessee Cavalry. Granddaughter Marie Blanche Duncan (1876–1958) is also buried in the plot.

In 1902, Mayor Hart purchased Magnolia Mound plantation house, built around 1815. Hart lived in a smaller house nearby while the main house deteriorated. His niece Marie Blanche Duncan purchased the estate in 1929, and by 1960, the house was uninhabited and neglected. When developers threatened to tear down the house, local citizens saved and restored it. (Courtesy of the Library of Congress.)

This beautiful monument over the grave of Henry C. Dearing (1856–1904) proclaims "Erected by the / Woodmen of the World." The WOW stones are referred to as "treestones" rather than headstones. This tree stump is split to symbolize a life ended. The stump sits on a stack of logs, a felled tree, while a lily grows out of the base to symbolize resurrection. The motto "*Dum Tacet Clamat*" (though silent, he speaks) is also included with the epitaph "Blessed are they that / mourn for they shall be comforted." In the left background, another WOW rough-hewn tombstone can be seen. In 1884, Dearing married Alice Eliza Coon (1868–1948), and they had three children. Dearing's mother was Helen A. Waddill Dearing (1825–1907), and his father was Dr. George Washington Dearing (1816–1882), whose office was in the drugstore of his father-in-law, H.T. Waddill, on Church Street.

Lilies and ivy encircle and adorn "to my / wife" on the bottom of a broken obelisk. Lilies represent purity and resurrection, and ivy represents immortality and fidelity. Ivy is believed to remain eternally green. When ivy is depicted clinging to a tree, it is a symbol of attachment and undying love.

This monument pairs an angel's finger holding the stems of lilies and roses with the words "Memory of my darling wife." Hardee G. Lambert erected this for his wife, Edna Cora Holt Lambert (1875–1914). Their son Hardell Lambert (?–1945) is nearby, and her parents, N. King Holt (1844–1911) and Cora Virginia Burnett Holt (1851–1890), are in an adjacent plot.

"My wife" is encircled by an elaborate wreath of flowers, and the stone is topped by a variety of flowers. Flowers are beautiful but quickly wilt and die, so they are symbols of the fleeting nature of human life. Roses represent love and the memory of Mary. Lilies represent purity, faithfulness, immortality, and fidelity. Carnations denote a woman's innocence.

George Alexandre Droz (1872–1929), once superintendent of the Baton Rouge post office, resigned to become a US Prohibition agent. He died after falling into a vat of boiling liquor during a raid in Jefferson Parish. Droz's tombstone consists of stacked logs with the WOW logo. His wife, Clotilde "Muz" A. Altazin Droz (1878–1964), is buried next to him.

Located in Section No. 4, Lot No. 37, the tombstone of David Cousin (1809–1878) reads, "In loving memory / of / David Cousin / city architect of / Edinburgh, Scotland / who died at Hermitage, / West Baton Rouge." Hermitage was a small community established around 1851 on the Mississippi River near the Pointe Coupee–West Baton Rouge Parish line. Cousin was known for designing important buildings in Edinburgh and was also involved in early cemetery design and landscape architecture. From 1841 to 1872, he served as Edinburgh's city superintendent of works (the city architect). His wife, Isabella Galloway Cousin (1804–1876), and he had three daughters, none of whom outlived their parents. Isabella is interred in Edinburgh. David Cousin retired to Louisiana. After Isabella's death, Cousin married Elizabeth Lawson (1826–1909) of Lanarkshire, Scotland. She is also buried in Magnolia and her inscription is on the back side of his grave marker. In his home Leith in Scotland, there is a monument to the Cousin family including David; his first wife, Isabella; their daughters; and his parents, who are buried there.

Dr. Richard Henry (1917–1973), "beloved father," was born in Guntersville, Alabama, and died in Marrero, Louisiana. The flowers and ivy leaves denote eternal life, and his profession is recognized by the medical staff. The adoption in 1902 of the caduceus for US Army medical officer uniforms popularized the use of the symbol throughout the medical field in the United States. The quote from Ecclesiastes is often placed on tombstones.

The Woodmen of the World logo shows a tree stump, which represents the end of life. The circle around the stump reads, "*Dum Tacet Clamat*," and is encircled by "Woodmen of the World Memorial." WOW is an insurance company established in the 1880s. Until the 1930s, it donated hand-carved tombstones for members when they died.

The "WC" on this tombstone refers to the Woodmen Circle, which began in 1892 as the ladies' branch of the Supreme Forest Woodmen of the World. Their purpose was to provide homes to orphans and widows of members of the WOW fraternal organization. The carving shows a crossed hammer and ax centered by a wedge, all tools of carpenters and other woodworkers.

The tombstone for William Oscar Kernan (1866–1905) and his wife, Winnie Booth Kernan (1868–1957), is a rough-hewn slab with a unique metal WOW plaque. Over time, the weathered metal has caused a stain down the tombstone. Kernan was a member of Manchac Lodge No. 3337, Knights of Honor, and WOW Live Oak Camp No. 17, as well as a bookkeeper for O.A. Bullion & Co.

According to local lore, these brick oven graves in Section No. 4, Lot No. 34, were moved from the Bernard family property in West Baton Rouge Parish at an unknown time. This early photograph shows the vaults in poor condition, but the bricks and original structure can still be seen. Later, the vaults were badly repaired. The Bernards were descendants of Onesiphor Bernard (1822–?), a prominent landholder and West Rouge Parish recorder, and his first wife, Zelamie Blanchard (1826–?), and his second wife, Delia Marie Dupuy Bauer Bernard (1837–1918). Delia and sons George Bernard (1878–1939) and Thomas Oscar Bauer (1857–1916) are buried in Magnolia but not in these graves. Few names are readable except for Isadore Bernard (1872–1912) and his wife, Lizzie L. Nelson Bernard (?–1914). A Joseph Bernard is buried in Section No. 3, Lot No. 1; he died in 1897 at age 65. Patsey Bernard is listed as the owner of Section No. 4, Lot No. 7. (Above, courtesy of the *Advocate*, Baton Rouge.)

Five

OUR DARLING BABY

"Our darling baby" is located in Section No. 5, Lot No. 59. No other angels stand near the beautiful, but sad, cherub over the grave of Ellen Claire Johnson, who was born July 28, 1944, and died November 13, 1948. Four-year-old Ellen had lived with her parents, George and Jane Ludwig Johnson, on Adams Avenue in Baton Rouge.

Charles William "Billy" Karney Sr. (1924–1973), Section No. 5, Lot No. 59, was a sergeant in the US Army. He was captured and reported as missing in action on October 1, 1944, and was finally returned from Korea in August 1951. His wife, Florieta "Flo" Bourgeious Karney (1924–2012), shares a headstone and the plot. "Loving memories last forever" is carved beneath enjoined hearts.

Lucie Lee Bates Marston (1871–1934), Section No. 5, Lot No. 31, and her husband, Joseph Graham Marston (1871–1953), moved to St. Louis, Missouri, but were returned for interment in Magnolia after their deaths. Lucie's parents and siblings are also buried in Magnolia Cemetery. Her father, John William Bates (1837–1909), served as parish sheriff from December 1878 to May 1888.

Turner Bynum Sr. (1878–1922), Section No. 5, Lot No. 35, was mayor of Baton Rouge at the time of his death. When Turner died unexpectedly of dengue fever, Wade Hampton Bynum (1868–1946) stepped in to finish his brother's term. The Bynum family home was on Laurel Street. Belle Hart Bynum (1878–1960), Turner's wife, was the niece of former mayor Robert Hart and active as a civic leader and pioneer businesswoman.

The Masons' symbols are shown in various ways throughout Magnolia Cemetery. The simplest ones, such as this grave maker, show only a line drawing of the well-known compass and level. Freemasonry is derived from the fraternal orders of stonemasons begun in the 14th century. Members are known as Freemasons or Masons, and their tombstones recognize their membership.

Frank Marion Womack (1893–1963) and his wife, Byrne Monget Womack (1895–1971), are buried next to each other in Section No. 5, Lot No. 25. Frank's family lived at Oaklawn Plantation in St. Helena Parish before the Civil War. He was a veteran of World War II, the first president of the Cadets of the Ole War Skule at LSU, and general manager of the Louisiana Bureau Filing Exchange. A precise but unadorned Masonic emblem is in the bottom center of his tombstone. Byrne was an alumni president at LSU, president of the Louisiana Federation of Business & Professional Women 1929–1932, and the society editor at the *Morning Advocate* and *State-Times*.

In contrast to simple emblems, this elaborate tombstone presents the Masonic symbol sculpted within a wreath of ivy suspended from a "brass" ring by distinctive ribbons. The square and compass, both architect's tools, joined together is the most identifiable symbol of Freemasonry and represents accuracy, integrity, and rightness. When the letter G appears within the compass, it stands for both God and Geometry. Often, the Masons performed rites at funerals and/or burials. Many graves throughout Magnolia Cemetery have Masonic emblems on them and emblems of the Order of the Eastern Star. Established in 1850, the Order of the Eastern Star was open to both men and women, although Eastern Star emblems are most often found on women's tombstones, such as that of Geneva Spinks Herbert (1870–1958). Soldiers' graves might, such as Claude Joseph Rordam's (1893–1939), display a Masonic emblem with American Legion emblems. The St. James Masonic Lodge No. 47 owns Lot No. 92 in Section No. 2, and the United Lodge No. 267 owns Lot No. 29 in Section No. 3.

JESSIE MOFFETT
LINDSAY
MAR. 29, 1900
FEB. 11, 1934

Four members of the Lindsay family are buried in Section No. 5, Lot No. 89. A mother and her three children all died on February 11, 1934, as the result of a gas leak in their home on Sandors Street in Capital Heights. Mother Jessie Moffett Lindsay (1900–1934), Jammie Audrie Lindsay (1918–1934), Victor K. Lindsay (1919–1934), and Billie Ruth Lindsay (1921–1934) had funerals and burials on February 13. The husband and father, James E. Lindsay, survived because he spent the night studying in the living room, where he kept a small heater burning and the doors to other parts of the house closed. Around 5:00 a.m., he opened a window in the bedroom and went to sleep, awaking in pain about 7:30 a.m. and discovering his family lifeless. He sought help from neighbor L.E. Causey.

JAMMIE AUDRIE
LINDSAY
JULY 15, 1918
FEB. 11, 1934

The newspaper headline of the *State-Times* on February 13, 1934, read, "Funeral Held for Victims of Gas Here: Mrs. James E. Lindsay and three children laid to rest as hundreds offer sympathy." Baton Rouge fire chief Robert A. Bogan reported that carbon-monoxide gas from the kitchen stove spread to the bedrooms. Attendance was so large that several hundred mourners were unable to be seated in the church and remained outside during the service at Emmanuel Baptist Church. The family had moved to Baton Rouge two years before from Selma, Louisiana, in Grant Parish for James E. Lindsay to attend LSU. At Emmanuel Baptist Church, he was a teacher of the young people's class and a choir leader, and he and his wife were active in the church's mission work.

This quiet plot has a family tombstone above the individual markers for the Lindsay family. Jammie was 16, Victor was 15, and Billie Ruth was 13 at the time of their deaths. Their grave markers are not monumental, such as that for the Crenshaw children who all died of yellow fever in 1858; however, the sadness at the loss of multiple children at the same time is just as poignant.

A lovely lamb tombstone has been broken from its base and never repaired. Young animals, particularly lambs, symbolize deceased children and their short lives. Many tombstone lambs are found in Magnolia Cemetery, and many are worn by time, such as this one. Other symbols for children's deaths are doves and a single rose on a broken stem.

Another monument to the loss of young children, the Bogan family obelisk memorializes "infants of / J.D. & C.E. Bogan / Douglas [(1899–1900)], / Harney / and / Eliza" on one side of the base. No birth and death dates are listed for Eliza, but Harney was born in 1902 and died in 1903, the same year his mother died. James Douglas Bogan (1864–1939), the father's name, is carved on another side of the base, and the mother's name is on another. Clara Elizabeth Sharp Bogan (1867–1903) was a native of Illinois. James D. Bogan was the president of the Bogan Realty Company, located at 217 Main Street for many years. In 1926, he and his second wife, Nan, lived with his and Clara's sons Samuel Skolfield Bogan (1895–1957) and Thaddeus Bogan (1899–1970) at 440 France Street. Samuel is buried in Magnolia near his parents, and Thaddeus is buried in Greenoaks Memorial Park, Baton Rouge.

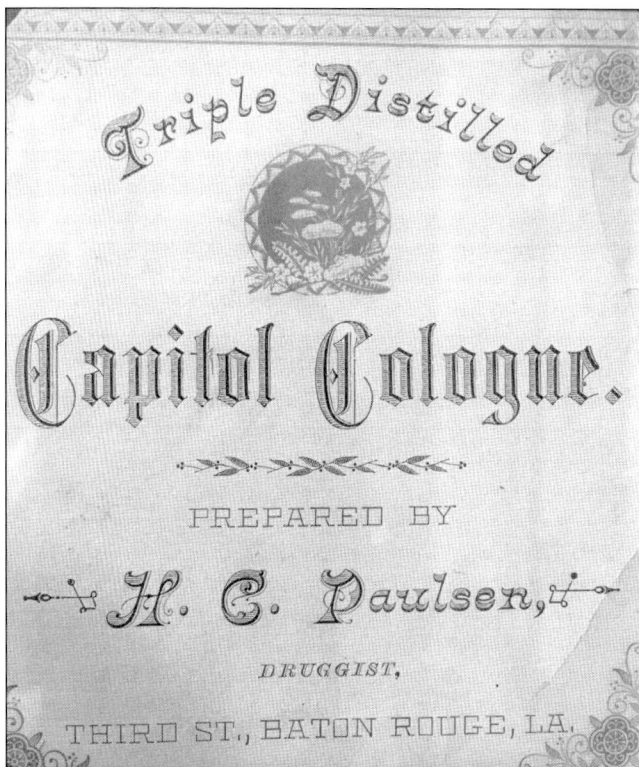

Triple Distilled

Capitol Cologne.

PREPARED BY

H. C. Paulsen,

DRUGGIST,

THIRD ST., BATON ROUGE, LA.

Hans C. Paulsen (1854–1923) came to New Orleans from Leck, Germany, in 1871 and began working as a druggist. Around 1880, Paulsen and his family came to Baton Rouge and opened a drugstore in the first block of Third Street. Druggists in the 19th century prepared their own medicines and other products in their stores. Paulsen created the products and designed labels for the bottles. In his drugstore in the capital city of Louisiana, he created "Capitol Cologne," presumably a fragrance, and "Capitol Cough," a medicine. He also created the formula for the well-known Paulsen's Heat Powder. (Left, courtesy of Vicki Hall.)

HANS C. PAULSEN
JUNE 6TH 1854
AUGUST 1ST 1923

Anna Marie Hansen Paulsen (1852–1930) was also born in Germany and married druggist Hans in 1877 in New Orleans. They had 10 children. Documented as buried near their parents in Magnolia Cemetery are Katie (1878–1969), Hans H. (1879–1948), Thomas Christian (1885–1951), Marguerite (1887–1957), and Josie Allison (1894–1895). The family home was at 602 Government Street. Sons Hans and Otto Paulsen (1891–1963) were engaged in the drugstore business with their father. Thomas became a medical doctor and maintained his office in the drugstore building. H.C. Paulsen and Son, Retail Druggists, remained at 301 Main Street into the late 20th century. (Right, courtesy of Vicki Hall.)

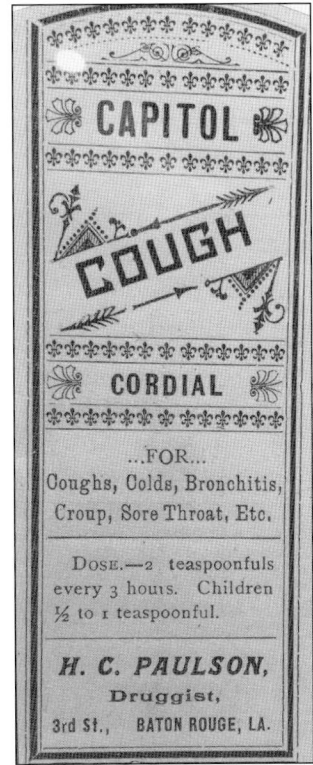

CAPITOL COUGH CORDIAL

...FOR...
Coughs, Colds, Bronchitis, Croup, Sore Throat, Etc.

DOSE.—2 teaspoonfuls every 3 hours. Children ½ to 1 teaspoonful.

H. C. PAULSON,
Druggist,
3rd St.,   BATON ROUGE, LA.

ANNA M. HANSEN
WIFE OF H.G. PAULSEN
1852 —— 1930

Resting lambs are most often seen on the tombstones of children, but some are found gracing the graves of adults. This lamb symbol represents "at rest" for Ella Brown Ivey (1881–1958). In some records, she is listed as Luella. Her tombstone lamb shows signs of weathering but has not been broken. Her husband's tombstone is next to hers. Charles W. Ivey (1873–1921) has the epitaph "gone but not forgotten" on his tombstone. Ella and Charles Ivey had two children, Mignon Ivey Paetz (1911–1996), interred in Baton Rouge's Roselawn Memorial Park, and Sidney Porter Ivey (1918–1999), interred in Baton Rouge's St. George Catholic Church Cemetery. Also in Roselawn is the son of Charles Ivey and his first wife, Elizabeth (1874–1903), Henry Francis Ivey (1896–1955). His tombstone bears the same epitaph as his father's Magnolia Cemetery tombstone.

By breaking the word brother into two parts, the stone carver was able to place "our / bro / ther" within the flower wreath on the front of this tombstone. The wreath of lilies is elaborately carved and tied together by a ribbon at the bottom.

William Joseph Ryan (1881–1954), Section No. 5, Lot No. 55, was a captain in the US Navy and served in the Spanish-American War, the Boxer Rebellion in China, and both World War I and II. As one of the first in Louisiana to receive a private pilot's license in 1932, he became an instructor. He is remembered most as the namesake for Baton Rouge's Ryan Airport.

Katherine Coleman Herget Huckabay (1900–2002), Section No. 5, Lot No. 38, is in the Herget family plot. She was voted the "most popular girl" at LSU in 1919, 1920, and 1921, the year she graduated. Katherine lived to be 101 years old. Her husband, Harry Hunter Huckabay (1900–1967), lies next to her. Also in the Herget family plot are Katherine's mother and father, two brothers, and two sisters.

Joseph Arthur Loret (1893–1970), Section No. 5, Lot No. 30, graduated from LSU in 1915 and became a Baton Rouge attorney. For several years, he served as the assistant attorney general of Puerto Rico. His first wife, Mary Belle Conrad (1872–1919), is buried in the lot with him. They lived on Boyd Avenue near the old LSU campus.

Many children's graves were adorned with doves to symbolize purity, loyalty, love, peace, and grace. The flying dove carrying a flower represents the soul being carried to heaven. Its color, white, represents purity and spirituality. Doves are an important animal in Christianity, also representing God's connection to earth.

Ollie Brice Steele (1884–1919), Section No. 5, Lot No. 33, was a captain in the 4th Kentucky Infantry during the Civil War. He was the patriarch of the Steele-Burden family, which includes Baton Rouge business owners and philanthropists. The family came to Baton Rouge in 1884 when Steele was elected state auditor. He also served as state treasurer and as an officer with the Bank of Baton Rouge.

Alvin C. Henderson (1925–1945), Section No. 5, Lot No. 64, served as a technician in the 341st Field Artillery Battalion during World War II and was killed in action in June 1945. His body was returned for a Magnolia Cemetery burial. His tombstone is engraved with a small cross. He and his family had lived on Greenwell Springs Road in East Baton Rouge Parish.

Pearlie Nesser Buckner (1894–1976) was the first female deputy sheriff in East Baton Rouge Parish and in the state of Louisiana, and the first woman deputy tax collector. Off Airline Highway in East Baton Rouge Parish is an area known as the village of Nesser where many of her family members were born. Her husband, Richard Aylette Bucker (1886–1920), is buried next to her.

Some of Magnolia Cemetery's statues are severely damaged. This Sacred Heart of Mary statue has lost her head and her right hand. She may also be lost from the original grave where she once stood. The position of her hands suggests that she was once carrying something. Vandals may be responsible for this damage. Mary and other saints are considered guardians of the dead and are often portrayed carrying flowers representing unfailing love and the restored innocence of the soul at death, scrolls representing the departed person's life being recorded, torches for life everlasting, a trumpet turned upside down signifying death, or swords depicting God's power. Statutes such as this became popular as tomb markers between 1850 and 1900. A family could have figures sculpted to order, which was expensive, or order standard items kept in stock by monument makers.

Robert Moon Walsh (1841–1896) attended Magruder's Collegiate Institute of Baton Rouge and served in the 2nd Louisiana Cavalry in the Civil War. Walsh's mother was a sister of A.E. McElhenny, the owner of Avery Island, and Walsh became a worker in the saltworks there. He also worked on a steamboat and held several government positions. His wife was Lena L. Mentz Walsh.

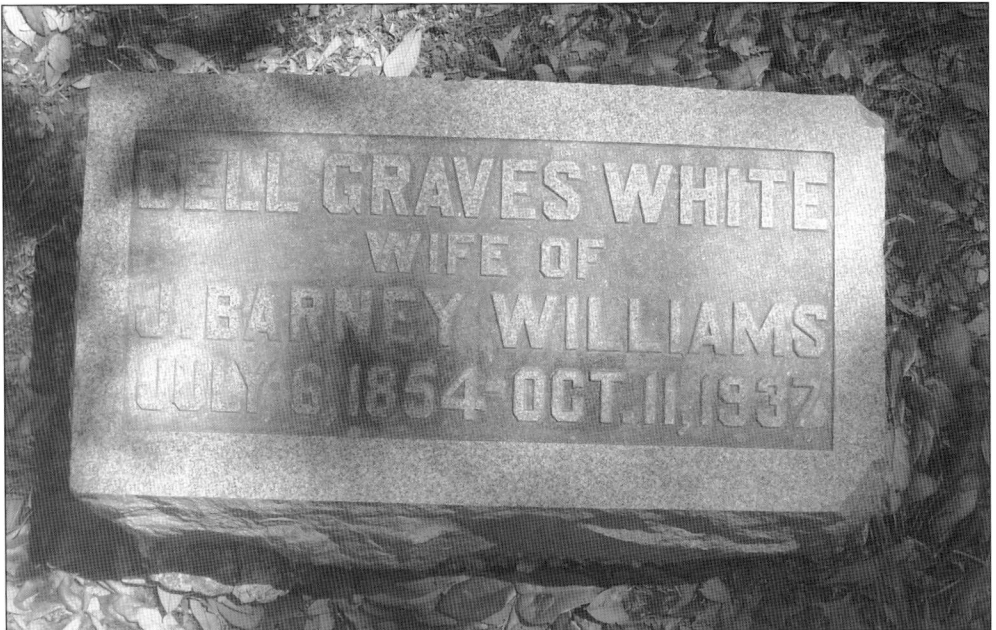

Bell Graves White Williams (1854–1937) was a member of the Baton Rouge Woman's Club and the Housewife's League and volunteered at the Baton Rouge General Hospital and the Protestant (Girls) Orphans home. Her husband, J. Barney Williams (1854–1918), rests next to her. His tombstone bears the emblem of the Woodmen of the World.

Six

HE LOVED GOD
AND HIS FELLOWMAN

Dr. Edward Oliver "Eddie" Powers (1864–1919) is in Section No. 6, Lot No. 58. His tombstone displays a Masonic symbol and the epitaph "He loved God and his fellow man." His wife, Johnnie Orvilla Nettles Powers Robinson (1872–1949), is buried next to him even though her second husband is buried in Mississippi where she died. Johnnie's and Edward's tombstones have matching ivy designs.

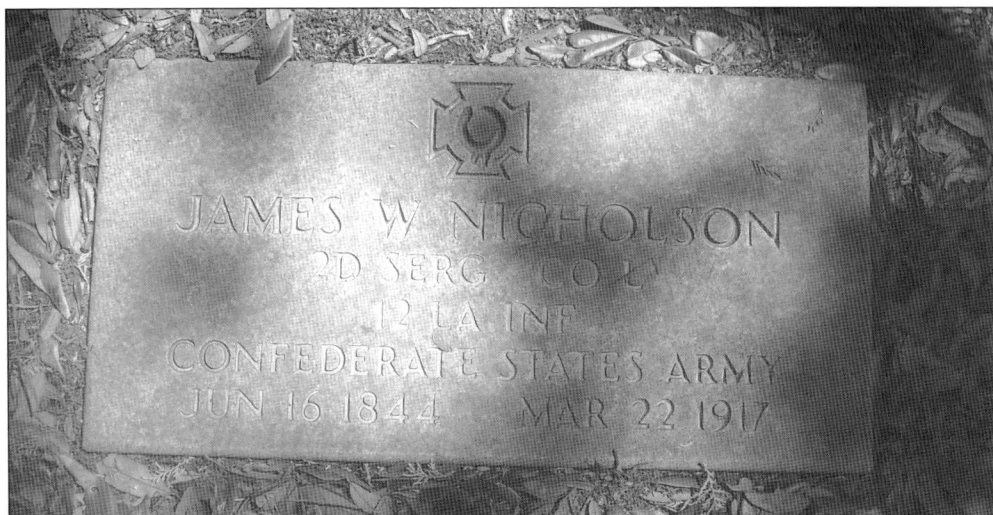

James William Nicholson (1844–1917), Section No. 6, Lot No. 20, served in the Civil War as a sergeant in Company L, 12th Louisiana Infantry, known as the Claiborne Rangers. Nicholson's grave is also marked by a Southern Cross of Honor. In 1889, he gave a eulogy at the funeral of Confederate president Jefferson Davis.

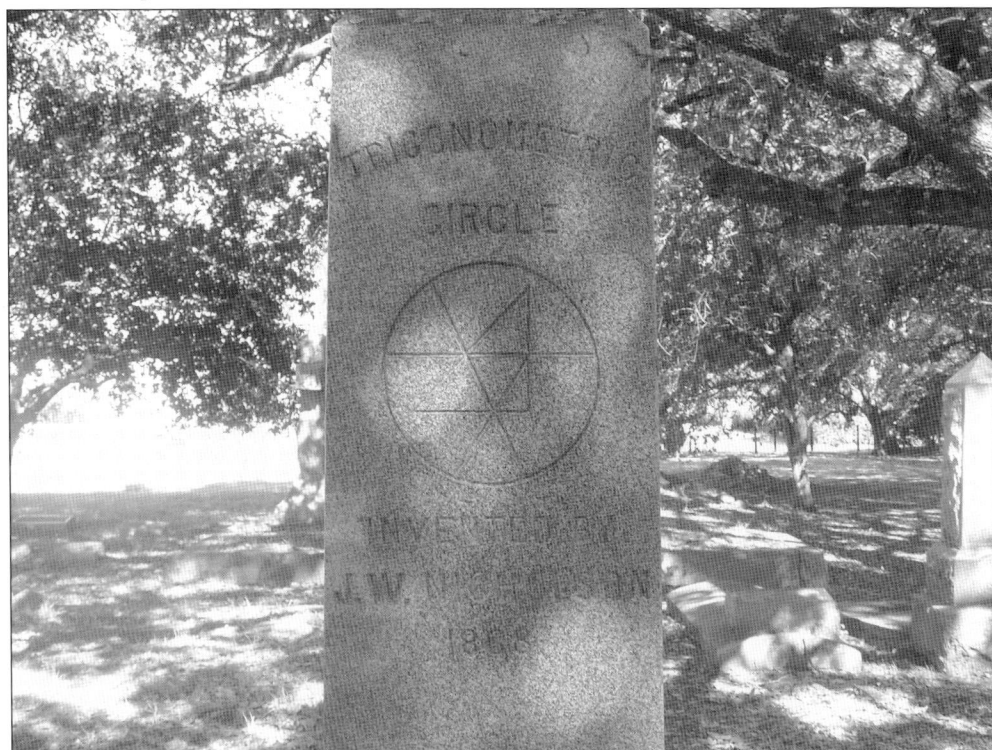

Nicholson was the longtime chairman of the LSU math department. In 1868, he published a pamphlet on the trigonometric circle, explaining his formula for expressing the relation between the sides and functions of the angles of right-angled triangles. The circle appears on his unique obelisk. His wife, Sallie D. Baker Nicholson (1859–1895), is buried by him and her name appears on one side of his obelisk.

Lilburne Nicholson Daspit (1879–1973), Section No. 6, Lot No. 20, was an honors graduate of Louisiana State University and, for 20 years, was a mathematics instructor there. Her father was mathematics professor and LSU president J.W. Nicholson. Her husband, Armand Pierre Daspit (1876–1956), is also buried in Lot No. 20.

J.W. Nicholson was a popular teacher and is pictured leading a mathematics class at LSU in 1899. At that time, all students at LSU were male cadets. Nicholson also served as president of the university twice, first from 1883 to 1884 and again from 1887 to 1896. (Courtesy of LSU Photograph Collection, 1886–1926, Louisiana State University Archives, LSU Libraries.)

Nolan Stewart Dougherty Sr. (1853–1912), Section No. 6, Lot No. 40, served as the East Baton Rouge Parish sheriff from 1904 through 1908. He also served as president of the Louisiana National Bank, as state representative for East Baton Rouge Parish (twice), and as secretary of the State Bureau of Agriculture in 1892, and was active in the Knights of Columbus. After his death, his family dedicated a stained-glass window to him in St. Joseph Catholic Church. He and his wife, Lilly McConnell Dougherty (1862–1917), married in 1881 and share the same headstone, located near a rough-hewn cross erected to the memory of all Dougherty family members buried in Lot No. 40. Dougherty was a descendant of Elvira Moore McCalop Stewart, the first owner of the historic Baton Rouge Stewart-Dougherty House at 741 North Street that served as a hospital for wounded Federal troops in 1862–1863.

Charles Phelps Manship (1881–1947), Section No. 6, Lot No. 60, took over control of the *State-Times* newspaper in 1909. It absorbed the *New Advocate*, from which the *Morning Advocate*, the first successful Baton Rouge morning newspaper, began in 1925. Manship created radio stations WJBO in 1933 and WBRL in 1941. Manship was also involved in local businesses and civic organizations. He married Leora Douthit (1882–1950) in 1904, and she is buried beside him.

Jules Roux (1868–1913), Section No. 6, Lot No. 39, was mayor of Baton Rouge at the time of his death. Roux was elected in 1910 and began transitions in the city administration to create broader representation. His reforms were continued by his successors. Family members buried in the lot are Marie C. Roux (1871–1950) and Rosalind Roux (1906–1925).

Edwin Hedge Fay (1832–1898) and his wife, Sarah Elizabeth Shields Fay (1837–1919), have matching rough-hewn tombstones. The rough stones resemble some Woodmen of the World markers, but there is no evidence that they were members. Her epitaph reads "rejoicing in hope / patient in tribulation," and his "Christ is my hope." They married in 1856 and had two daughters, Sara Elizabeth Fay Morgan (1870–1958), who is buried in Knoxville, Tennessee, and Lucy E. Fay (1875–1963), also buried in Knoxville near her sister. Both Edwin's and Sarah's stones bear an anchor. The anchor was regarded in ancient times as a symbol of safety and was adopted by Christians as a symbol of hope and steadfastness. Edwin served as superintendent of education in Clinton, Louisiana, until his death. During the Civil War, he served in Captain Webb's company, Louisiana Cavalry.

The paupers' section is along the Main Street fence at the top of Section No. 6. Originally, in 1852, one quarter of the cemetery was set aside for the burial of the poor and unknown. In the 21st century, the designated space has no room for new caskets; therefore, coroners have remains cremated and scatter them in the paupers' section.

It is hard to read the words and to interpret the snake-like lines on this homemade tablet atop a dome grave cover. It is next to a small stone for carpenter Burrell Luther Caster (1885–1932) and his wife, Nellie Caster (?–1932).

When money was not available to purchase a headstone, a family member or friend of the deceased might create a personal, folk art–type grave marker. Throughout Magnolia Cemetery, personally created grave markers can be found. For example, this handmade cross marks the grave of Lenoria Tucker "at rest."

A toppled cross lies near the grave of Carl Ray Bennett (1936–1975), whose veterans' marker states that he was a private in the US Marine Corps and served in Korea. It is not known if the cross belonged to his grave, but it could have been erected for someone as a temporary marker.

This monument is a large tree-like obelisk with Masonic emblems at the top, followed underneath by a cross and crown, and then a large centered cross and the Brooks name below a flowered base. In the plot are Francis Marion Brooks (1844–1891) and his wife, Egeria Lorena Willis Brooks (1845–1932), as well as daughter Alma Egeria Brooks (1873–1944) and granddaughter Egeria "Cherie" Brooks Barnett (1895–1974). In the Civil War, Francis Marion Brooks was a private in Company B, 1st Louisiana Cavalry, and a hospital steward. He became a prisoner of war in 1863 and was released in 1865. The large monument marks his grave. Francis Marion's father was Eri Morley Brooks Sr. (1824–1874), a second lieutenant in Company B, 1st Louisiana Cavalry, and he too became a prisoner of war. The Brooks plot retains its marble and wrought iron enclosure in fair condition.

Thomas Duckett Boyd (1854–1932), Section No. 6, Lot No. 37, and his brother David French Boyd both served as early presidents of Louisiana State University, and their names are synonymous with LSU. From 1896 until 1926, Thomas Boyd, pictured at left, served as president and was responsible for establishing the law school and the College of Education, and for admitting women as students in 1904. He earned undergraduate and master's degrees from LSU and a law degree from Tulane University. His wife, Annie Foules Fuqua (1858–1931), and their children, Thomas Duckett Boyd Jr. (1882–1964), Minerva "Minnie" French Boyd Howell (1888–1973), Overton Fuqua Boyd (1892–1951), and Henry Cecil Boyd (1895–1914), are also buried in the family plot. (Left, courtesy of LSU Photograph Collection, Louisiana and Lower Mississippi Valley Collections, LSU Libraries.)

On All Saints' Day, November 1, students from nearby schools often participate in the annual cleanup of Magnolia Cemetery. Here, student members of the Alpha Phi Omega sorority at Louisiana State University clean graves and place fresh flowers on them in remembrance of the dead. (Courtesy of the *Advocate*, Baton Rouge.)

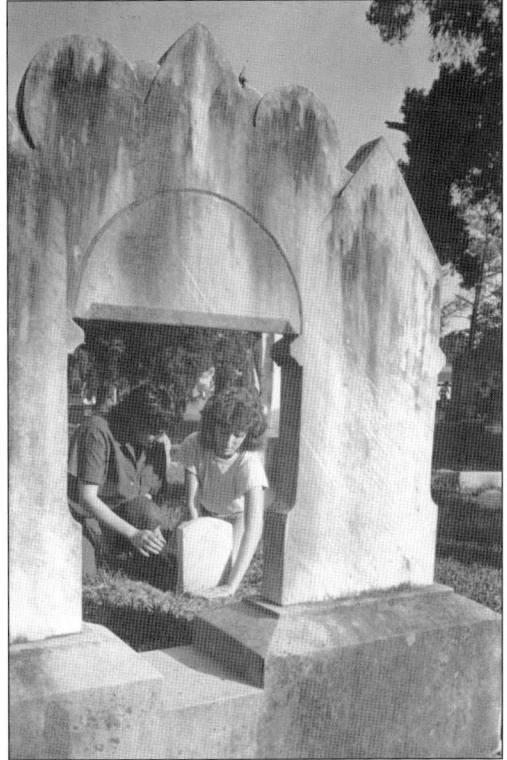

Samuel B. Swift (1848–1926), Company I, 3rd Iowa Cavalry, US Army, and his wife, Laura Jane (1852–1947), are buried next to each other. They lived near Plank Road, so named because it was a road covered by wooden planks. Beginning in the mid-1800s, plank boards were laid over muddy roadways on log foundations, greatly helping local travel, and many still existed when the first cars became popular.

SAMUEL SWIFT
CO I 3 IOWA CAVALRY
CIVIL WAR
JUL 2 1926

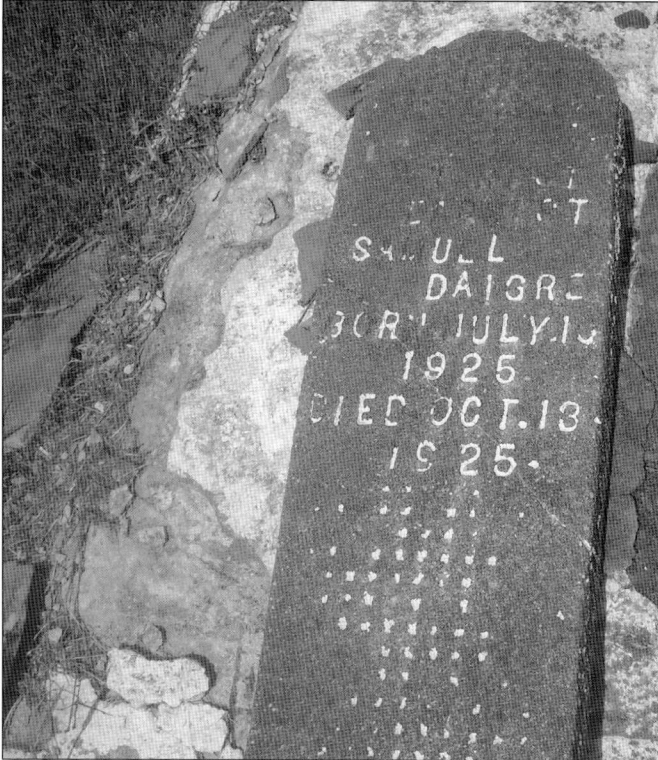

The tombstone of infant Earnest Samuel Daigre (July 16 to October 18, 1925) appears handmade from concrete. It is near the graves of many other Daigre family graves in a plot owned by Ida Daigre (1902–1939). The Daigres were a well-known family.

The unique rectangular coping (the stone on the outside of the plot) around the grave of Andres Cantu (1915–1923) appears to have once had flower vases or similar items on each side. These have been lost over time, but the large cross remains sturdy. If other members of young Andres's family are buried in Magnolia, they have not been located.

Seven

BLESSED ARE THE PURE IN HEART

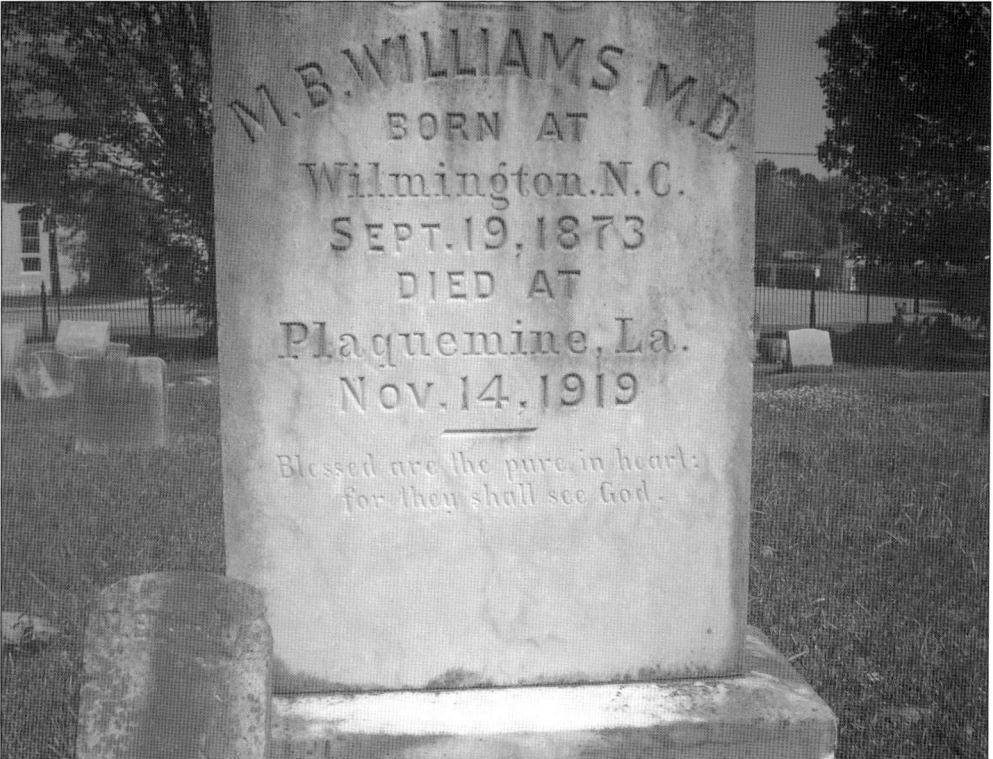

M.B. Williams (1873–1919) was a native of Wilmington, North Carolina. Dr. Williams died at Plaquemine, Louisiana, and was brought to Magnolia Cemetery for burial. His headstone bears a lamp of life, symbolizing death, with a scrolled ivy vine on each side, symbolizing resurrection. It bears the epitaph "Blessed are the pure in heart: / for they shall see God."

Magnolia Cemetery does not have perpetual care, so families or organizations must maintain the graves. After the Civil War, Baton Rouge's economy failed. Families who had once cared for the resting places of loved ones could no longer afford maintenance and repairs. Later, as remaining family members moved away from Baton Rouge communities, Magnolia Cemetery continued to fall into disrepair. Now, some graves are so damaged that the occupants can no longer be identified, and they are thought of as the "unknowns." The Historic Magnolia Cemetery Board of Trustees and Preserve Louisiana, as well as other community groups, hold cleanup days and encourage citizens to help maintain the cemetery.

No matter the type of covering above the graves, neglect leaves the elements to do their worst on them. This brick single vault should have an inscription denoting its occupant, but if an identification was once there, it has been worn away by weeds and rain. The identity of the occupants of these three raised blanket vaults that touch each other is unknown. The two in the rear are not broken; however, the front blanket covering seems to have been smashed by something. Even in concrete, plants will grow and make cracks larger and more open to rain.

Vera Marino and her grandson often come to Magnolia Cemetery on November 1, All Saints Day, to clean and place flowers on the graves of family members as well as others. In Louisiana, family traditions to celebrate All Saints Day include visiting, cleaning, repairing, and leaving flowers on the graves of relatives and friends, as well as holding vigils and reading scriptures at the graves. (Courtesy of the *Advocate*, Baton Rouge.)

Lavinia Smiler of the Myrtle Wheat, Household of Ruth, died June 8, 1913. Her tombstone's engraving shows that it was "Presented by the Members of / District Grand Household of Ruth No. 26," a women's organization of the Grand United Order of Odd Fellows in America. Smiler and her family were listed as living at 1842 North Street in the 1913 city directory.

The oven vault of the Independent Order of Odd Fellows Desoto Lodge No. 7 contains on the far right the grave of Arthur Edmond Rice (1888–1953). Odd Fellows tombstones are marked with three interlocking rings—a chain—showing "FLT," which signifies friendship, brotherly love, and truth. They own Lot No. 112 in Section No. 4. Madeline Forrester (died November 8, 1938) is also in the Odd Fellows Plot, Desoto Lodge.

The monument of Bell R. Webster (1870–1892) bears the inscription "In Memory of / Bell R. Webster / only son of / J.S. Webster / and / Orella Lambremont . . . He loved the good and all the / good loved him." His monument is topped by a large urn symbolizing immortality. After the cross, the urn is one of the most commonly used cemetery monuments. Another side bears the sentiment "who made his grave a wilderness / of flowers."

117

Alexander Douglass Barrow (1838–1903) served as a colonel in Company C, 9th Louisiana Battery. Barrow and his wife, Lise Victorine Duralde Barrow (1839–1893), have beautiful monuments to mark their graves. His is a large cross that was broken in two places but has been repaired, and hers shows lilies, representing faithfulness, and a rose, representing love and immortality, carved in a large circle. The circle is known as the symbol for eternal life and never-ending existence. They were married in 1859. Colonel Barrow was born in West Feliciana Parish, the son of Wylie Micajah Barrow (1810–1853) and Cordelia G. Johnston Barrow (1816–1845), who are also buried in Magnolia Cemetery. Barrow was killed in a ferryboat accident while crossing the Mississippi River to Baton Rouge from his home in Port Allen where he was a well-known plantation owner.

These sad, forgotten graves show how much damage can happen over time to graves that are neglected. Damage can be caused by storms, fallen branches, excessive rainwater, and even vandals. Bits and pieces of several box tombs are pushed together, making it impossible to determine which piece belongs to which grave.

Although the base of a missing gravestone lies next to the grave of Michael Dewayne Beauregard (1956–1979), no evidence remains to identify whose headstone once sat atop it. The headstone could have been broken by a falling tree during a storm. Headstones and monuments have also been damaged by automobiles pushed into the cemetery by collisions on the surrounding streets.

Members of the Reeder family are buried together. This broken monument is for Rebecca Rue Reeder (1788–1851), born in Virginia, and her husband, Daniel Foster Reeder (1780–1853). Their first son was born in Ohio and their second in Louisiana around 1817. Rebecca and Daniel died in East Feliciana Parish. Near their graves are William Andrew Reeder Sr. (1869–1958), Nell Roberta Reeder (1873–1956), and Sarah Jane Reeder (1864–1954).

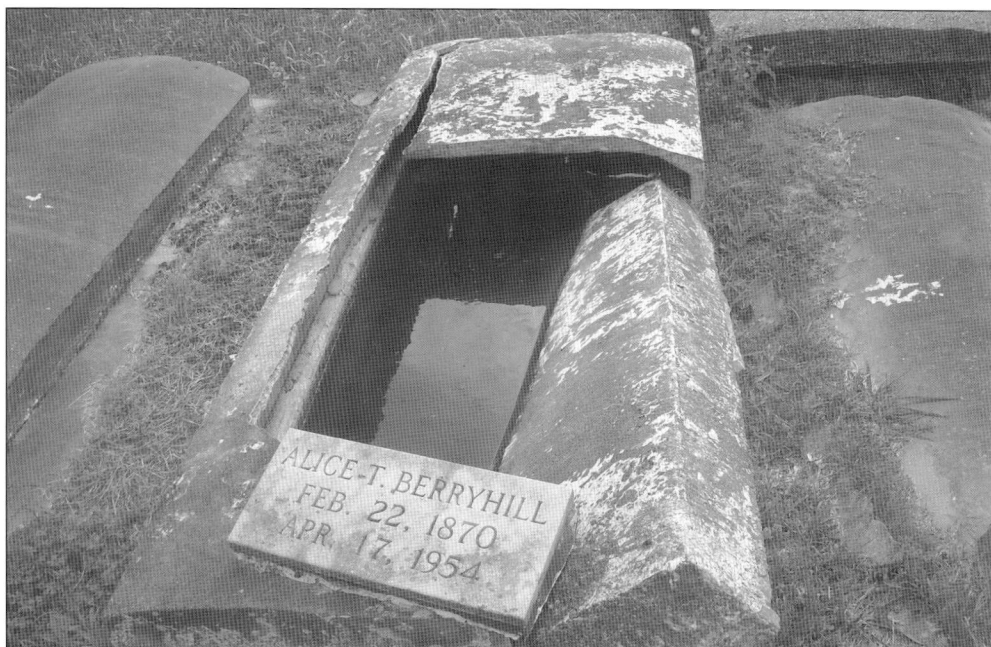

It is hard to believe that a mound grave from 1954 could be in such disrepair as that of Alice Thomas Berryhill (1870–1954). It is unknown how the concrete cover was broken. Without repairs to close the hole, rainwater will continue to erode the contents of the grave. A stone for Jacob Berryhill (1862–1928) is nearby.

Critical to the beauty of Magnolia Cemetery were the talents of stonemasons, but most have been forgotten. However, many monuments do show stonemasons' names engraved near their bases. In 1907, the Fraternal Order of Elks published its *Elks Souvenir of Baton Rouge* booklet containing advertisements by local businesses, including Baton Rouge's Fridge Marble Works; Alonzo A. Fridge (1859–1933) was its proprietor. (Courtesy of the East Baton Rouge Parish Library.)

Some non-Louisianian stonemasons who are identified in Magnolia and other Baton Rouge cemeteries include "Enochs, Phila," a company based in Philadelphia, Pennsylvania. Such companies probably offered not only made-to-order works but also a catalog of available completed works, such as the wide variety of angels and crosses found in most cemeteries in the 19th and 20th centuries.

Stonemasons from outside Baton Rouge created many tombstones and monuments for Magnolia Cemetery and other local cemeteries. Acme Marble & Granite Company of New Orleans is another company whose logo appears often on tombstones in Magnolia Cemetery. Backes Marble & Granite Works of New Orleans advertised in the July 8, 1911, issue of the *Donaldsonville Chief* and listed its address as 318 Baronne Street. The Dean logo does not identify the company's location. Hannan & Voss is another example of a company that created tombstones found in Baton Rouge. The work of these stonemasons was installed in Baton Rouge cemeteries from the 1880s through the 1980s.

Magnolia Cemetery monuments reflect styles of cemetery art from the 1850s with many symbolic uses of flower images and realistic human figures. Such individualized monuments were installed until the late 20th century, when the majority became stock monuments. Stock monuments are created in mass productions not directly associated with an individual grave. The Dean monument company and the company of Hannan & Voss did original hand-sculpted grave makers as well as mass-produced items. In a 1911 newspaper advertisement, Backes Marble & Granite Works encouraged customers to write for a catalog of monuments in stock at their warehouse.

A headless Sacred Heart of Mary stands near the graves of members of the Thiel and Nephler families. Saints shown writing in an open book are known as scribers and symbolize the accounting of the deceased's life before God. Damage has also occurred to the top of the tombstone for Mary Nephler (1824–1892). Nearby is the tombstone for Mary's husband, Francis A. Nephler (1823–1904), and to his left is one for baby Florence Edna Thiel (1881–1883) marked with a lamb and a rose bud with a broken stem. Two other babies are also buried here, Beatrice Iola (died August 2, 1870, at two days old) and Blanche Irene (died September 28, 1870, at two months, eleven days). The connection between the two families is the marriage of Emma C. Nephler (1849–1927) to Charles Augustus Thiel (1841–1904), who served as a Union captain during the Civil War in Company M, 4th Missouri Cavalry.

There is a tombstone in Magnolia Cemetery for Capt. Benjamin Franklin Burnett, Company B, 9th Battery, Louisiana Cavalry, but no birth and death dates are engraved on it. Records do show that Burnett enlisted on May 15, 1862. Near Captain Burnett's tombstone is a vault that is unidentifiable because of its extensive damage.

Throughout Magnolia Cemetery many unusual and unique tombstones have been erected. A member of the Duplessis family has a stone with an open book at the center top, symbolizing the Bible and/or a person whose good life is an open book. Ivy, a symbol of eternal life, spills down the side. At the bottom is the epitaph "at rest." Nearby is a stone for William Duplessis (1844–1907).

The Sacred Heart of Mary near the graves of the Thiel and Nephler families is shown here before her head was lost. She gently looks down toward the graves and to the book in which she is writing. Her writing symbolizes the deceased's name being included in the Book of Life, ensuring them a place in Heaven. (Courtesy of the East Baton Rouge Parish Library.)

The dove that once sat atop the tombstone of two-year-old Louie Ward Perkins (1905–1907) has lost its head and wings, and its tail is also damaged. His parents, W.H.&M. Perkins, may have chosen a dove for his tombstone because it symbolizes love and the promise of everlasting life.

Ironworkers such as "R. Pike, Maker, 1011 Poeyfarre St., NO, LA," also added to the beauty of Magnolia Cemetery. Pike, the fence maker of the 1909 wrought iron fence for Magnolia, had his workshop in what is now known as the New Orleans Warehouse District. Many different fences surround family lots, but not many of the fence makers are identified.

The main drive through Magnolia Cemetery features a view of a canopy of trees from the entrance gate on Nineteenth Street. In addition to its namesake magnolia trees, the land designated for the cemetery contained live oak trees. Caretakers encouraged the live oaks to grow into a canopy, adding more or new trees as necessary.

DISCOVER THOUSANDS OF LOCAL HISTORY BOOKS FEATURING MILLIONS OF VINTAGE IMAGES

Arcadia Publishing, the leading local history publisher in the United States, is committed to making history accessible and meaningful through publishing books that celebrate and preserve the heritage of America's people and places.

Find more books like this at
www.arcadiapublishing.com

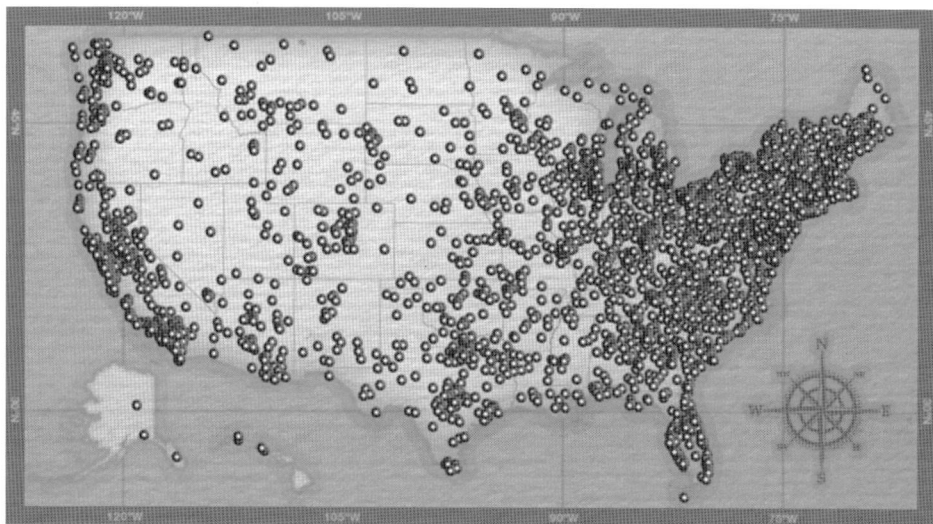

Search for your hometown history, your old stomping grounds, and even your favorite sports team.